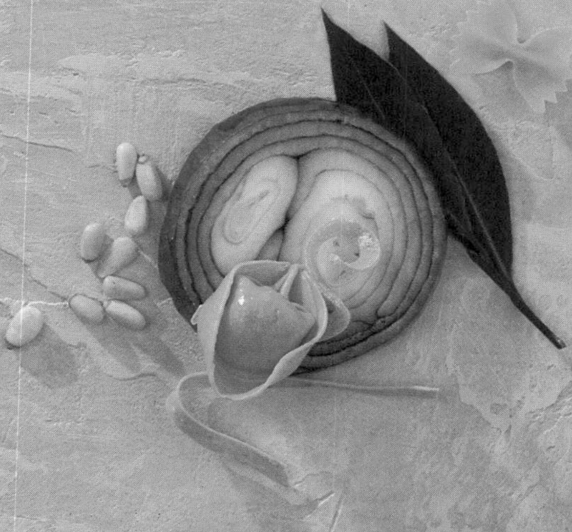

BECCA WATSON'S
PERFECT PASTA

BECCA WATSON'S
PERFECT
PASTA

MEREHURST

To Mum and Dad, with love

Published in 1996 by Merehurst Limited
Ferry House, 51-57 Lacy Road, Putney, London SW15 1PR

ISBN 1-85391-566-1

Editor: Maureen Callis
Series Designer: Roger Hammond
Photographer: Ken Field
Food prepared for photography by: Louise Pickford
Assisted by: Carol Tennant
Stylist: Marian Price
Typesetter: Michael Weintroub

Colour separation by Fotographics Ltd UK, Hong Kong
Printed in Singapore by CS Graphics Pte Ltd

NOTES

Cooking times for pasta vary enormously. Always follow packet instructions – my times are a guide only.

Add 1 tablespoon salt to boiling water when cooking pasta. This is not listed in ingredients.

Everything is cooked over medium heat unless high, low or cook gently are specified.

Add sauce to pasta and toss together off heat unless stated otherwise.

Pasta names are given in Italian. English versions are only given
if the Italian name is not very well known.

A standard spoon measurement is used in all recipes:

1 teaspoon = one 5 ml spoon   1 tablespoon = one 15 ml spoon

All spoon measures are level.

Ovens should be preheated to the specified temperature.

For all recipes, quantities are given in metric and imperial. Follow one set
of measures but not a mixture as they are not interchangeable.

*Frontispiece: Fresh Penne with Roasted Peppers (right), see page 45,
and Spaghetti Pescatore (left), see page 65*

FOREWORD

Like fish on Friday, I was brought up with spaghetti bolognaise every Wednesday, so it could be said that I am no stranger to pasta. Over the last eleven years I have been making up for lost time (after all, you can only eat so much spaghetti bolognaise!) and experimented with the hundreds of varieties of pasta available, making sauces to match. This is the result of my experiments by trial and error.

When I was first approached to write this book, I thought about how I would like it laid out. I am rarely restricted by ingredients when cooking for friends, as most of them will eat just about anything, but what I do find restricting is lifestyle.

I've learnt from experience that there is always someone who is dieting and more often than not a vegetarian in the midst. At other times, when I'm a bit broke, I want recipes that don't cost the earth. When my parents come to stay, I like to make a bit of an effort and cook something special and when I'm cooking for a crowd I want something that can be made in advance. Also, when I'm working I like to rush home from the office and prepare something to eat within half-an-hour and not have a lot of washing-up at the end of it!

I'm sure you will be able to relate to at least four if not all of the seven chapters in this book. I have included a chapter on classic pastas as sometimes you can't beat what you already know. I'm a strong believer that a certain comfort is gained from familiarity – rather like nursery puddings.

Many of these recipes have been collected from friends and restaurants that I have worked in. I have been inspired by dishes eaten on holidays and in some of the better restaurants I have visited. I have taken the ideas and developed them according to my own taste. There are no hard and fast rules when it comes to pasta, so I hope you will pluck from this collection those you like and develop them to suit your own personal tastes.

I have never been a great one for making fresh pasta – more through laziness than anything else. However, there are many varieties of good quality fresh pastas on the market now, which I have included in the recipes. Whether you prefer to use fresh, dried, or homemade I will leave up to you.

Testing the recipes for this book was much easier than I'd expected and made me reach the conclusion that pasta is idiot-proof, as the friends who helped me are far from professional cooks! My thanks go to my Mum, Bridget, Gemma, Michael, Chris, Steve, Coralie, Penny and Lucy, whose comments were at times critical, but valued.

I do hope you enjoy reading this book as much as I have enjoyed writing it and I hope it will encourage you to experiment with different shapes of pasta and sauces.

Becca

Introduction

Light and low

Quick and easy

Simply vegetables

The classics

Something special

Budget pasta

Party pasta

INTRODUCTION

Pasta is probably one of the most versatile foods of our time. It's good for you, tastes of whatever you fancy and cooking it is not beyond anyone who can boil an egg. It is inexpensive, quick to cook and perfect for today's healthy lifestyle.

Furthermore, with the increasingly wide range of choices available – from green, red or wholewheat to fresh pasta flavoured with garlic and herbs, not to mention the endless variety of dried shapes – pasta can never be boring.

Most of the recipes in this book will serve four as a main course. Bread and simple side salads are an optional accompaniment – I like to serve bread to soak up the sauce. The only exceptions are the Party Pasta recipes which serve eight and the Quick and Easy recipes which serve two, leaving you to halve or double up the ingredients as you please.

With the exception of the fresh filled pasta dishes, dried, fresh or homemade pasta can be used in all the recipes. It really boils down to convenience and what you have in the cupboard or close at hand.

The word pasta simply means dough in Italian but is used to describe penne, spaghetti, lasagne and the many other pasta shapes which are made from the basic dough mixture. It is said that in Italy there are enough kinds of pasta to serve a different one every day, although only about fifty of them are well known. Elsewhere the choice is narrower but there are still a great many from which to choose, both fresh and dried.

Many people think that fresh pasta is more authentic than dried, but that isn't necessarily true. It's more a case that fresh pasta has become quite trendy, so more and more varieties are being produced. In southern Italy, the home of dried pasta, huge quantities are still being made and sold – and you can't get more authentic than that!

There are two types of dried pasta: one made with egg and one simply with water. Pasta made with egg is usually yellower in colour and, I think, superior to those made without. The best commercially dried pasta is made with 100% durum wheat so look for this or *pasta di semola di grano duro* on the packet.

Whether you use fresh or dried is really a matter of personal taste and time. If time is short I use fresh pasta – particularly the fresh filled tortellini and ravioli types which I recommend. I find some of the longer varieties can be a bit stodgy, so I would opt for dried in those instances.

Pasta can be long, short, thin, wide, flat, ribbed or tubular, to mention just a few types, and certain shapes lend themselves better to certain sauces. As a general rule, use the fine long pasta – spaghetti, tagliatelle and vermicelli – with thin sauces that have a smooth texture. The larger shapes – rigatoni, penne and fusilli – go well with meat and chunkier sauces. In a recipe that has a lot of sauce use shells or tubes, as they hold the sauce well. In other respects the choice is yours – wholewheat, tomato, spinach, egg – the world's your oyster.

THE LONG AND SHORT OF IT
The variety of shapes and sizes of pasta is enormous and sometimes confusing. I have seen the same pasta called two completely

different names in separate shops. These are the most commonly used shapes, all of which appear in this book.

Pasta	Other Names
Campanelle	Flutes
Cannelloni	
Cappelletti	Little hats
Casarecce	Gemelli, fine twists
Cavatappi	Corkscrews
Conchiglie	Shells
Conchigliliette	Maruzze
Couscous	
Ditali	Small macaroni
Farfalle	Bow ties
Fettucine	Small ribbons/Trenette
Fiorelli	
Fusilli	Twists
Lasagne	
Linguini	Thin narrow ribbons
Lumaconi	Big snails
Macaroni	
Orecchiette	Little ears
Paglia e fieno	Green and yellow noodles
Pappardelle	Wide ribbons
Penne	Quills
Pipe	Elbow macaroni
Ravioli	
Riccioli	Twists
Rigatoni	Tubes
Spaghetti	
Spaghettini	Thin spaghetti
Tagliarini	Fine fettucine
Tagliatelle	Noodles
Tortellini	Crescents
Trenette	Fine Noodles
Vermicelli	

COOKING PASTA

There are a few general rules to follow when cooking pasta to be sure of success.

Whether using fresh or dried, pasta needs a lot of water when cooking. The general rule is 2.5 litres (4 pints) water for 250 g (8 oz) pasta. If you use too little water, the pasta will stick to itself and the bottom of the pan.

Bring the water to a rolling boil in a large deep saucepan. Add 1 tablespoon salt. Add the pasta, stir once and cook uncovered at a steady boil, so that the pasta does not stick together. Cook until *al dente* – literally meaning 'to the tooth', tender but still with a bite – then add a couple of tablespoons cold water to the pan to stop it cooking any further.

Drain the pasta in a colander, add immediately to the sauce and toss together until well coated. Be sure to use cooked pasta at once, as directed, because it will stick together if left to stand. Never rinse it unless it is to be used for a salad, in which case you should rinse it under running cold water.

Take care not to overcook pasta. Fresh pasta needs only the briefest cooking time, so watch it carefully. I have given guides to cooking times for all of the recipes, but they should be used only as guides. Make sure you refer to the packet instructions.

HOW MUCH TO SERVE

For an average main meal portion, allow 50 to 125 g (2 to 4 oz) dried and 75 to 150 g (3 to 5 oz) fresh pasta per head, depending on the type used. Allow 175 to 200 g (6 to 7 oz) fresh filled pasta like tortellini.

Light and low

Pasta is not fattening, as many people believe – it is usually the fat content of the sauces that sends the calories sky high. When cooked, a generous 125 g (4 oz) portion only contains about 150 calories. If you steer away from butter, cream and full-fat cheese sauces, pasta can become a real friend as part of a weight-reducing diet or simply a healthy lifestyle. These recipes will not make you slim, but they are good for you.

LINGUINI WITH MUSHROOM SAUCE

Time to make: 15 minutes
Time to cook: about 15 minutes

Serves 4

1 onion

1 clove garlic

250 g (8 oz) open cup mushrooms

150 g (5 oz) oyster mushrooms

150 g (5 oz) shitake or chestnut mushrooms

1 tablespoon olive oil

300 g (10 oz) dried linguini

3 tablespoons chopped fresh parsley

250 ml (8 fl oz) dry white wine

salt and freshly ground black pepper to taste

250 ml (8 fl oz) Greek-style yogurt

One of the worst things about dieting is craving the foods you feel deprived of, like cream sauces. This recipe, packed with mushrooms and coated in a creamy yogurt sauce, will hopefully rid you of those cravings. There are hundreds of different varieties of mushrooms available, so use the quantities as a guide and choose mushrooms according to your personal taste and availability.

1 Chop the onion and crush the garlic. Finely chop the open cup mushrooms. Slice the oyster, shitake or chestnut mushrooms.
2 Heat the oil in a large saucepan, add the onion and garlic and cook gently for 5 minutes until soft.
3 Meanwhile bring a large saucepan of salted water to the boil, add the linguini and cook according to packet instructions until tender, which should take about 10 minutes.
4 Add the chopped mushrooms to the onion and cook for 4 minutes until they begin to soften. Add 2 tablespoons of the parsley and the wine. Bring to the boil, then lower the heat and simmer uncovered for 2 to 3 minutes until the wine has almost evaporated.
5 Add the sliced mushrooms and season with salt and ground black pepper. Cover and simmer gently for 5 minutes until the mushrooms are just tender.
6 Drain the linguini and immediately return it to the pan. Stir in the yogurt. Add the mushroom mixture and toss lightly together. Check seasoning and sprinkle with the remaining parsley to serve.

Adding the mushroom mixture to the linguini

MEDITERRANEAN PASTA SALAD

Time to make: 20 minutes
Time to cook: 10 to 15 minutes

Serves 4

---

175 g (6 oz) dried tricolour fusilli (3-colour twists)

2 tomatoes

1 red pepper

¼ cucumber

4 spring onions

125 g (4 oz) feta cheese

50 g (2 oz) pitted black olives

Dressing

4 tablespoons lemon juice

1 tablespoon clear honey

1 teaspoon dry English mustard

salt and freshly ground black pepper to taste

Ever since an idyllic two-week holiday spent on Symi, a remote Greek island, I've been a real fan of Greek salad. I have to admit it's the feta cheese and olive oil that I really enjoy, which isn't ideal when I'm trying to lose weight ready for the next bikini-bound holiday! However, much as I try I cannot give up feta, so I've developed this Greek-inspired pasta salad which includes feta cheese but with a fat-free dressing – all for under 300 calories a serving.

1   Bring a large saucepan of salted water to the boil, add the fusilli and cook according to packet instructions until tender, which should take about 12 minutes.
2   Meanwhile preheat the grill to high. Quarter and seed the tomatoes, then cut the quarters in half again. Put in a salad bowl. Quarter, core and seed the red pepper and put skin side up in the grill pan. Grill for about 5 minutes until the skin is blistered and charred. Put in a plastic bag for 2 minutes to loosen the skin, then peel and cut the flesh into strips. Add to the bowl.
3   Cut the cucumber into 1 cm (½ in) chunks. Slice the spring onions. Cut the cheese into 1 cm (½ in) cubes. Drain the fusilli and refresh under running cold water. Add the cucumber, spring onions, cheese and fusilli to the salad bowl and mix well.
4   To make the dressing: put the lemon juice, honey, mustard and seasoning in a screw-top jar and shake until mixed. Stir into the salad until the pasta, vegetables and cheese are well coated. Scatter the olives over the top and serve.

Cook's Tip
If you are counting fat units and not calories, allow 50 to 75 g (2 to 3 oz) pasta per person.

FARFALLE WITH PRAWNS, TOMATO, GARLIC AND PARSLEY

Time to make: 5 minutes
Time to cook: 10 to 15 minutes

Serves 2

175 g (6 oz) dried farfalle

2 fat cloves garlic

1 teaspoon olive oil

250 g (8 oz) shelled prawns

salt and freshly ground black pepper to taste

8 tablespoons passata

2 tablespoons chopped fresh parsley

I have adapted this recipe from my favourite starter at Piermasters restaurant in Plymouth. Stephen Williams, the chef, cooks giant prawns in butter with garlic, tomato and parsley and delicious it is too! I have replaced the butter with a little olive oil and used small shelled prawns as they mingle well with the pasta. You could add a little white wine, which is completely fat-free, if you find the sauce too dry.

1   Bring a large saucepan of salted water to the boil, add the farfalle and cook according to packet instructions until tender, which should take about 12 minutes.
2   Finely chop the garlic. Five minutes before the farfalle is cooked, heat the oil in a small frying pan over low heat. Add the garlic and cook, shaking the pan, for 30 seconds until the garlic whitens.
3   Remove the pan from the heat. Add the prawns and season with salt and ground black pepper. Add the passata and parsley. Return to the heat and bring to the boil, then lower the heat, cover (use a plate if you don't have a lid) and simmer gently for 1 minute until the prawns are heated through but still plump, not shrunken.
4   Drain the farfalle and immediately return it to the pan. Add the prawns, tossing the mixture together until the farfalle is well coated with the sauce. Serve at once.

Cook's Tip
Passata is sieved tomatoes, sold in bottles or cartons in supermarkets. If you can't get it, simply empty a can of chopped tomatoes into a plastic sieve, discard the juice and press the flesh through the sieve. Do not use a metal sieve as the acid from the tomatoes will react with the metal. Alternatively, put the flesh in a blender or food processor and process until smooth, then pass through a sieve to remove the seeds. You may find you need to add a pinch of sugar to the tomatoes, as passata is slightly sweeter than canned tomatoes.

MINESTRONE SOUP

Time to make: 35 minutes plus
  overnight soaking
Time to cook: 2 hours 25 minutes

Serves 6

125 g (4 oz) dried haricot beans

2 onions

2 carrots

2 small potatoes

1 stick celery

1 leek

¼ small green cabbage

2 rashers smoked back bacon

2 cloves garlic

1 tablespoon olive oil

2 tablespoons chopped fresh mixed herbs

125 ml (4 fl oz) red wine

397 g (14 oz) can chopped tomatoes

1.75 litres (3 pints) vegetable stock

salt and freshly ground black pepper to taste

50 g (2 oz) dried macaroni

This classic soup, originally from Milan but with many variations around the Mediterranean, is brilliant for staving off hunger pangs. I often make double quantities and keep it in the fridge for when I get in from work starving – a warm mug-full stops me picking on biscuits! It makes a great meal in itself too. If you are vegetarian simply leave out the bacon and substitute more vegetables – almost any vegetables can be added and any amount of different small pasta shapes too. There are no rules when it comes to Minestrone so experiment with whichever flavours of vegetables you like.

1   Put the beans in bowl, cover with cold water and leave to soak overnight.
2   Finely chop the onions, carrots and potatoes. Thinly slice the celery and leek. Finely shred the cabbage. Remove the rind and any fat from the bacon then dice. Crush the garlic.
3   Heat the oil in a large saucepan, add the onion, garlic, bacon and herbs and fry for 3 minutes, then cover and cook gently for 5 minutes, stirring occasionally, until soft. Add the carrots, celery and leek and cook for 3 minutes, until beginning to soften.
4   Add the wine, bring to the boil then lower the heat and simmer for 2 minutes until reduced by half. Drain the beans and add to the pan with the tomatoes and stock. Bring to the boil, then lower the heat, cover and simmer for 1½ hours. Add the potato and season with salt and ground black pepper. Simmer gently for a further 15 minutes. Add the macaroni and cabbage and cook for a further 25 minutes until the beans are tender.
5   Check seasoning and serve in warmed soup plates.

Cook's Tip
If you're not dieting, serve this soup with a spoonful of pesto and sprinkle with freshly grated Parmesan cheese.

PENNE WITH SUN-DRIED TOMATOES AND CHICKEN

Time to make: 20 minutes plus
    soaking time
Time to cook: about 35 minutes

Serves 4

2 dried, sun-dried tomatoes

8 tablespoons boiling water

175 g (6 oz) skinned chicken breast fillet

4 tablespoons dry white wine

3 tablespoons chopped fresh basil

1 large shallot

2 cloves garlic

5 pitted black olives

125 g (4 oz) button mushrooms

125 g (4 oz) frozen petit pois or fresh peas

salt and freshly ground black pepper to taste

250 g (8 oz) dried penne

1 teaspoon olive oil

pinch of crushed chillies

1 tablespoon plain flour

300 ml (10 fl oz) skimmed milk

pinch of freshly grated nutmeg

Entertaining on a diet isn't always easy as I hate the thought of subjecting my guests to a noticeably low calorie dish and depriving them of delicious foods. This recipe gets around the problem really well. It's smart enough to serve to friends, filling, delicious and very low in fat – your guests never need know you're slimming.

1 Set the oven to 180C, 350F, Gas 4. Put the sun-dried tomatoes in a small mixing bowl, pour over the boiling water and leave to soak for 20 minutes until reconstituted, then drain.

2 Remove any visible fat from the chicken. Put the chicken in a shallow ovenproof dish with the wine and 1 tablespoon of the basil. Cover and cook in the centre of the oven for 15 to 20 minutes until the meat is white and the juices run clear when the chicken is pierced with a skewer

3 Meanwhile finely chop the shallot and crush the garlic. Thinly slice the olives and sun-dried tomatoes. Slice the mushrooms.

4 Pour the cooking juices from the chicken into a saucepan. Add the shallot, mushrooms, tomatoes and peas. Season with ground black pepper. Bring to the boil, then lower the heat, cover and simmer gently for 5 minutes, stirring occasionally. Set aside.

5 Bring a large saucepan of salted water to the boil, add the penne and cook according to packet instructions until tender, which should take about 12 minutes.

6 Meanwhile slice the cooked chicken. Heat the oil in a saucepan, add the garlic and crushed chillies and cook for 30 seconds, shaking the pan, until the garlic whitens. Add the flour and milk and cook for 3 minutes, whisking constantly until the sauce has thickened. Stir in the nutmeg and season with salt and ground black pepper. Return the chicken and vegetables to the pan, cover and simmer gently for 2 minutes.

7 Drain the penne and immediately return it to the pan. Add the sauce and remaining basil and toss over low heat until the penne is well coated. Sprinkle with the sliced olives to serve.

FETTUCINE WITH CURRIED CHICKEN

Time to make: 20 minutes
Time to cook: 25 to 30 minutes

Serves 4

2 onions

3 cloves garlic

2.5 cm (1 in) piece root ginger

1 small green pepper

1 small red pepper

250 g (8 oz) skinned chicken breast fillet

2 teaspoons oil

½ teaspoon fenugreek seeds

½ teaspoon onion seeds

397 g (14 oz) can chopped tomatoes

1 teaspoon ground coriander

1 teaspoon curry powder

1 teaspoon salt

2 tablespoons lemon juice

4 tablespoons chopped fresh coriander

300 g (10 oz) dried fettucine verdi

coriander leaves to garnish

When the novelty of dieting begins to wear off and my willpower is waning, I always treat myself to this curried chicken pasta to get me back on the straight and narrow. Curries are usually very high in fat as traditionally they use a lot of oil in the cooking process, but this one is a tomato-based sauce with a minimal amount of oil. So next time you get the urge to dial a curry, don't – try this recipe instead. It has all the flavour of a good curry, but is good for you too!

1   Finely chop the onions and crush the garlic. Peel and finely chop the root ginger. Halve, core, seed and dice the green and red peppers. Cut the chicken into 1 cm (½ in) chunks.
2   Heat the oil in a saucepan, add the fenugreek and onion seeds and cook gently for 1 minute. Add the onion, garlic and ginger and cook gently for 5 minutes, stirring occasionally, until the onion is golden.
3   Meanwhile pour the tomatoes into a mixing bowl, add the ground coriander, curry powder, salt and lemon juice and mix well. Add to the pan and bring to the boil, stirring occasionally. Lower the heat and simmer gently for 3 minutes.
4   Add the peppers and chicken and cook over a medium heat for 7 minutes, stirring occasionally.
5   Add the chopped coriander, cover and simmer over low heat for 10 minutes.
6   Meanwhile bring a large saucepan of salted water to the boil, add the fettucine and cook according to packet instructions until tender, which should take about 10 minutes.
7   Drain the fettucine and immediately return it to the pan. Add the sauce, tossing gently until the fettucine is well coated. Garnish with coriander leaves to serve.

FUSILLI WITH BROCCOLI AND SUN-DRIED TOMATOES

Time to make: 10 minutes
Time to cook: 10 to 15 minutes

Serves 4

350 g (12 oz) broccoli

1 yellow pepper

125 g (4 oz) small chestnut mushrooms

4 sun-dried tomatoes (see Cook's Tips below)

2 cloves garlic

350 g (12 oz) dried fusilli

1 teaspoon olive oil

300 ml (10 fl oz) vegetable stock

3 tablespoons chopped fresh mixed herbs (oregano, rosemary, coriander, mint, thyme)

pinch of dried chilli flakes

150 ml (5 fl oz) white wine

salt and freshly ground black pepper to taste

2 tablespoons freshly grated Parmesan cheese

Garnish

mixed herb sprigs

Parmesan cheese shavings (see page 28), optional

Top: Casarecce with Grilled Red Peppers, Saffron and Basil (see page 20)

Bottom: Fusilli with Broccoli and Sun-Dried Tomatoes

This recipe comes from my local Italian restaurant, Bianco Verdi. The secret ingredients are the mixed herbs which are chopped fresh every night. The packets of fresh mixed herbs now available in supermarkets are ideal for this recipe and a lot cheaper than buying five different varieties of fresh herbs.

1   Cut the broccoli into bite-size florets. Quarter, core, seed and thinly slice the yellow pepper. Slice the mushrooms. Rinse and drain the sun-dried tomatoes on absorbent kitchen paper and slice very thinly. Crush the garlic.

2   Bring a large saucepan of salted water to the boil, add the fusilli and cook according to packet instructions until tender, which should take about 12 minutes.

3   Meanwhile heat the oil in a large frying pan, add the garlic and fry for 30 seconds, shaking the pan, until the garlic whitens. Stir in 150 ml (5 fl oz) of the vegetable stock, the chopped mixed herbs and chilli flakes. Lower the heat and simmer until the stock has reduced by half.

4   Stir in the wine and simmer until reduced by half. Add the broccoli, yellow pepper, mushrooms and sun-dried tomatoes. Season with ground black pepper. Cover with a tight-fitting lid and cook for 4 minutes, stirring occasionally.

5   Drain the fusilli and return it to the pan. Add the vegetables, remaining vegetable stock and grated Parmesan cheese. Increase the heat and cook for 1 minute, stirring occasionally, until most of the liquid has evaporated and the fusilli is mixed with the vegetables. Check seasoning and garnish with herb sprigs and Parmesan cheese shavings if you wish. Serve at once.

Cook's Tips

Use dried sun-dried tomatoes if you can get them, as they are obviously lower in fat. (See page 16 for preparation.) If you cannot get them, use the variety in oil but rinse and drain them well on absorbent kitchen paper before use.

Use a pan with a tight-fitting lid so that the vegetables practically steam themselves, releasing their juices into the sauce.

CASARECCE WITH GRILLED RED PEPPERS, SAFFRON AND BASIL

Time to make: 25 minutes
Time to cook: 15 to 20 minutes

Serves 4

1 red pepper
1 yellow pepper
2 large tomatoes
pinch of saffron threads
2 tablespoons boiling water
1 large red onion
3 cloves garlic
1 handful of basil leaves
1 tablespoon olive oil
300 g (10 oz) dried casarecce
300 ml (10 fl oz) semi-skimmed milk
1 tablespoon crème fraîche
2 teaspoons cornflour
salt and freshly ground black pepper to taste
1 tablespoon freshly grated Parmesan cheese to serve

Photographed on page 19

O nce a year I try and escape to a health farm for a couple of days to relax and get away from it all. When I'm not fasting there's always plenty of wonderful fresh healthy food to choose from. This recipe is one I was given at Grayshott Hall and is more like a meal you'd be served in a restaurant than on a diet! It has just 350 calories per serving with a medium fat content.

1   Preheat the grill to high. Put the whole peppers in the grill pan and grill for about 10 minutes, turning occasionally, until the skins are blackened on all sides. Put in a plastic bag for about 5 minutes to loosen the skins.

2   Plunge the tomatoes into a bowl of boiling water for 30 seconds. Remove with a slotted spoon and peel away their skins, then halve, seed and chop.

3   Put the saffron threads in a small mixing bowl and cover with the boiling water. Leave to soak.

4   Finely chop the onion and crush the garlic. Tear the basil into shreds. Halve, core and seed the peppers, then peel off their skins. Cut the flesh into 1 cm (½ in) strips.

5   Heat the oil in a saucepan, add the onion and garlic and cook for 5 minutes, stirring occasionally, until the onion is golden.

6   Meanwhile bring a large saucepan of salted water to the boil, add the casarecce and cook according to packet instructions until tender, which should take 10 to 12 minutes.

7   Pour the milk into a mixing bowl, add the crème fraîche and cornflour and whisk together.

8   Add the pepper strips to the onion and cook for 1 minute, stirring occasionally. Add the tomatoes, saffron threads and soaking liquid, bring to the boil, then lower the heat and simmer gently for 2 minutes.

9   Add the milk mixture to the pan, bring to the boil, then lower the heat and simmer until the sauce has reduced by one-third. Stir in the basil and season with salt and ground black pepper.

10   Drain the casarecce thoroughly and return it to the pan. Add the sauce, tossing gently until the casarecce is well coated. Check seasoning and transfer to warmed serving plates. Sprinkle with the Parmesan and serve at once.

SPAGHETTI WITH GARLIC, CHILLI AND LEMON

Time to make: 10 minutes
Time to cook: about 15 minutes

Serves 4

1 large fresh red chilli

4 cloves garlic

1 lemon

125 g (4 oz) watercress

300 g (10 oz) dried spaghetti

1 teaspoon olive oil

8 tablespoons dry white wine

2 tablespoons freshly grated Parmesan cheese

salt and freshly ground black pepper to taste

During my holidays from college I used to work as a waitress in Piermasters restaurant in Devon. This spaghetti dish is a low-fat version of one that the chef used to serve up for staff lunch. I have replaced much of the oil with white wine to reduce the fat and have chosen spaghetti, although linguini, fettucine and tagliatelle are all suitable alternatives.

1 Seed and finely chop the chilli and crush the garlic. Finely grate the rind and squeeze the juice from the lemon. Tear the watercress into shreds.
2 Bring a large saucepan of salted water to the boil, add the spaghetti and cook according to packet instructions until tender, which should take about 15 minutes.
3 Meanwhile heat the oil in a large frying pan, add the garlic and chilli and cook for 3 minutes, stirring occasionally, until the garlic is golden.
4 Remove the frying pan from the heat and add the wine. Return to high heat and cook for 2 minutes until the wine has reduced by half.
5 Drain the spaghetti and transfer it to the frying pan. Add the watercress, lemon rind and juice, and Parmesan cheese. Season with ground black pepper and toss together until the spaghetti is coated with the sauce. Serve at once.

Cook's Tip
Tossing cooked pasta in a little chicken stock before adding the sauce lends the same silky texture as olive oil but with none of the fat. The stock lubricates the pasta and stops them sticking together.

Quick and easy

As the pace of life has increased, fast food has become essential in today's busy lifestyles. But because it has to be quick doesn't mean it should be short on taste or nutritional value. Pasta is ideal – full of goodness, it becomes something really tasty with a simple sauce. Those in this chapter can all be made in half-an-hour – some in just 15 minutes – and will provide endless inspiration to busy cooks looking for a quick supper.

SPAGHETTI WITH SESAME, BROCCOLI AND CORN

Time to make: 20 minutes
Time to cook: about 15 minutes

Serves 2

175 g (6 oz) dried spaghetti

2 tablespoons sesame seeds

250 g (8 oz) broccoli

1 clove garlic

1 small fresh red chilli

4 spring onions

2 teaspoons sesame oil

1 teaspoon fresh ginger purée

125 g (4 oz) baby corn

2 tablespoons honey

2 tablespoons dark soy sauce

2 tablespoons dry sherry

salt and freshly ground black pepper to taste

A friend gave me a wok for my eighteenth birthday and ten years on, although battered and blackened, it's still serving me well. I've adapted this recipe from one of my old faithful stir-fry recipes of broccoli and corn with sesame seeds. I usually serve it with Chinese noodles, but find that spaghetti and tagliatelle work just as well.

1 Bring a large saucepan of salted water to the boil, add the spaghetti and cook according to packet instructions until tender, which should take about 15 minutes.
2 Meanwhile put the sesame seeds in a frying pan and dry-fry for 2 minutes, stirring occasionally, until golden brown. Remove from heat and set aside.
3 Cut the broccoli into florets. Crush the garlic and seed and finely chop the chilli. Thinly slice the spring onions.
4 Heat the oil in a wok or large frying pan, add the garlic, chilli, spring onions and ginger purée and stir-fry for 2 minutes. Add the broccoli and corn and cook for a further 2 minutes.
5 Mix together the honey, soy sauce and sherry. Stir into the wok, toss well and cook for a further 2 minutes until the vegetables are tender but still crisp. Sprinkle in the sesame seeds.
6 Drain the spaghetti and add to the wok. Season with salt and ground black pepper and toss well to mix. Serve at once.

Adding the spaghetti to the broccoli and corn mixture in the wok

CAPPELLETTI WITH SOFT CHEESE & WHITE WINE SAUCE

Time to make: 5 minutes
Time to cook: 20 to 25 minutes

Serves 2

125 g (4 oz) button mushrooms

175 g (6 oz) Brie or Camembert

25 g (1 oz) butter

6 tablespoons dry white wine

6 tablespoons double cream

salt and freshly ground black pepper to taste

200 g (7 oz) dried cappelletti

1 tablespoon chopped fresh parsley

This quick and easy recipe was created by Ben Frow, alias Paul Smortions, in his Small Portions cookery booklet, featured on TV's 'This Morning' programme. The recipe is the result of a vegetarian friend turning up unexpectedly for supper when all Ben had in his fridge were mushrooms and cheese. I've used cappelletti – the pasta which looks like top hats or tummy buttons, depending which way you look at them – but you could use penne, tagliatelli or fusilli.

1   Slice the mushrooms. Trim the rind from the Brie or Camembert and discard. Slice the cheese.
2   Melt the butter in a saucepan, add the mushrooms and cook for 3 minutes, stirring occasionally, until they begin to soften. Add the cheese, wine and cream. Season with salt and ground black pepper.
3   Bring to the boil, stirring, then lower the heat and simmer uncovered for 20 minutes until the cheese has melted and the sauce is a deep creamy colour.
4   Meanwhile bring a large saucepan of salted water to the boil, add the cappelletti and cook according to packet instructions until tender, which should take about 15 minutes.
5   Drain the cappelletti and immediately stir it into the sauce. Check seasoning, add the parsley and toss until the cappelletti is well coated with the sauce. Transfer to warmed serving plates and serve at once.

Cook's Tip
For a variation, substitute the Brie or Camembert with 175 g (6 oz) cream cheese with garlic and herbs.

THAT PASTA DISH

Time to make: 5 minutes
Time to cook: 10 minutes

Serves 2

1 small onion
2 cloves garlic
6 tablespoons olive oil
salt and freshly ground black pepper to taste
250 g (8 oz) fresh garlic and herb tagliatelle
125 g (4 oz) freshly grated Parmesan cheese

More taste less speed may be the motto that some cooks stand by, but there are times when I can't get out of the kitchen fast enough! That's when I take the attitude that the simpler you make things the better they taste, and in many cases it is true. This recipe couldn't be easier and always goes down well. In fact, whenever my friend Haig invites his friends from Scotland to stay, they only accept on the condition that he cooks 'that pasta dish' as it has now become known! You can also serve this sauce with penne or rigatoni.

1 Finely chop the onion and crush the garlic. Heat the oil in a frying pan, add the onion, garlic and plenty of salt and ground black pepper. Cook over low heat for 10 minutes, stirring occasionally, until the onion has softened.
2 Meanwhile bring a large saucepan of salted water to the boil, add the tagliatelle and cook according to packet instructions until tender, which should take 3 to 4 minutes.
3 Drain the tagliatelle and immediately return it to the pan. Add the onion and Parmesan cheese and toss together until well mixed. Transfer to warmed serving plates and serve at once.

Cook's Tip
To warm plates or bowls, put them in a washing-up bowl and pour over a kettle of boiling water. Leave for a couple of minutes, rinse and dry.

TAGLIATELLE WITH FETA, PLUM TOMATOES AND BASIL

Time to make: 15 minutes
Time to cook: 10 to 15 minutes

Serves 2

2 plum tomatoes or other flavourful tomatoes

1 red onion

1 clove garlic

125 g (4 oz) feta cheese

2 tablespoons olive oil

½ teaspoon sugar

½ teaspoon salt

250 g (8 oz) fresh tagliatelle

freshly ground black pepper to taste

2 tablespoons chopped fresh basil

basil leaves to garnish

2 teaspoons freshly grated Parmesan cheese to serve

This is another of my standard home-from-work suppers as I am lucky enough to have a delicatessen opposite my bus stop which stays open until 8 pm. They usually have a good supply of fresh plum tomatoes and basil, and as I'm addicted to feta cheese I've usually got some in the fridge. You could use other tomatoes, but you may need to add a little tomato purée to the sauce to compensate for the flavour lacking in some tomatoes.

1 Plunge the tomatoes into a bowl of boiling water for 30 seconds. Remove from the water with a slotted spoon and peel away their skins, then halve, seed and chop.
2 Finely chop the onion and crush the garlic. Roughly chop the feta cheese into 1 cm (½ in) cubes.
3 Heat the oil in a large saucepan, add the onion and garlic and cook for 2 minutes, stirring occasionally. Add the sugar, salt and tomatoes and cook over low heat for 10 minutes until the onion and tomatoes have softened .
4 Meanwhile bring a large saucepan of salted water to the boil, add the tagliatelle and cook according to packet instructions until tender, which should take 3 to 4 minutes.
5 Add the feta cheese to the sauce and season with ground black pepper. Cook for 1 minute until the cheese begins to melt. Remove from heat.
6 Drain the tagliatelle and immediately return it to the pan. Add the sauce and chopped basil, tossing the mixture gently together until well mixed. Transfer to warmed serving plates, garnish with basil leaves and sprinkle with the Parmesan cheese to serve.

Cook's Tip
Chop the feta cheese straight from the fridge as it is easier to cut when cold – it tends to crumble when it reaches room temperature.

Top: Fusilli with Five-Herb Sauce (see page 28)

Bottom: Tagliatelle with Feta, Plum Tomatoes and Basil

FUSILLI WITH FIVE-HERB SAUCE

Time to make: 10 minutes
Time to cook: 10 to 15 minutes

Serves 2 as a main course
or 4 as a starter

175 g (6 oz) dried fusilli

1 fat clove garlic

25 g (1 oz) butter

1 tablespoon snipped fresh chives

1 tablespoon chopped fresh basil

1 tablespoon fresh marjoram leaves

1 tablespoon fresh oregano leaves

1 tablespoon chopped fresh parsley

4 tablespoons dry white wine

salt and freshly ground black pepper to taste

Garnish

mixed herb sprigs

Parmesan cheese shavings (see Cook's Tip)

Photographed on page 26

This light pasta sauce makes a great starter as it has a fresh flavour which cleans the palette ready for the next course. It must be made using fresh not dried herbs. If you can only get three or four out of the five, just use those. The packets of mixed herbs from supermarkets often contain these five herbs, but be sure to sift out any bay leaves, thyme or rosemary as they would too overpowering.

1   Bring a large saucepan of salted water to the boil, add the fusilli and cook according to packet instructions until tender, which should take about 12 minutes.
2   Meanwhile crush the garlic. Melt the butter in a saucepan, add the chives, basil, marjoram, oregano, parsley and garlic and cook for 1 minute, stirring occasionally.
3   Pour in the wine and bring to the boil, then lower the heat and simmer gently, uncovered, for 4 minutes. Season with salt and ground black pepper.
4   Drain the fusilli and immediately return it to the pan. Add the herb sauce and toss together until well mixed. Transfer to warmed serving plates and garnish with herb sprigs and Parmesan cheese shavings. Serve at once.

Cook's Tip
Parmesan cheese shavings make a pleasant change to grated Parmesan for garnishing or serving with a pasta dish. To make, simply use a potato peeler to pare a 50 g (2 oz) piece of Parmesan cheese.

RIGATONI PIZZAIOLA

Time to make: 10 minutes
Time to cook: 15 to 20 minutes

Serves 4

2 cloves garlic
500 g (1 lb) sirloin steak
4 tablespoons olive oil
4 tablespoons chopped fresh mixed herbs – coriander, mint, thyme, rosemary, chives, parsley
1 large onion
150 ml (5 fl oz) red wine
397 g (14 oz) can chopped tomatoes
2 tablespoons tomato purée
½ beef stock cube
salt and freshly ground black pepper to taste
350 g (12 oz) dried rigatoni
50 g (2 oz) pitted black olives
4 tablespoons freshly grated Parmesan cheese to serve

My brother Ian is a real meat-and-two-veg man. When he comes to visit me I cook him this dish – strips of sirloin steak in a rich tomato and red wine sauce. As I've been eating less and less red meat over the past couple of years, I really enjoy this on the rare occasions that I have it as it seems a real treat. The recipe originally came from Bianco Verdi, my local pasta haunt.

1 Crush the garlic. Cut the steak into 1 cm (½ in) slices and put in a shallow dish with half of the garlic, 2 tablespoons of the oil and 2 tablespoons of the herbs. Toss together, cover and set aside.
2 Finely chop the onion. Heat the remaining 2 tablespoons oil in a large saucepan, add the onion and remaining garlic and fry for 4 minutes, stirring occasionally, until the onion begins to soften.
3 Add the wine and simmer gently, uncovered, until reduced by half. Add the chopped tomatoes, tomato purée and remaining herbs. Crumble the stock cube into the pan and season with ground black pepper. Bring to the boil, stirring constantly, then lower the heat and simmer gently for 10 to 15 minutes until the sauce thickens.
4 Meanwhile bring a large saucepan of salted water to the boil, add the rigatoni and cook according to packet instructions until tender, which should take about 13 minutes. Cut the olives into quarters.
5 Five minutes before the rigatoni is ready, heat a large non-stick frying pan. Add the steak and cook for 3 minutes, stirring occasionally, until sealed. Remove from the pan with a slotted spoon and add to the tomato sauce with the olives.
6 Drain the rigatoni and immediately return it to the pan. Add the sauce and toss together until the rigatoni is well coated. Sprinkle with the Parmesan cheese and serve at once.

Cook's Tip
If you have more time, or are organized in the mornings, marinate the meat during the day or overnight so that it has longer to absorb the flavours and become really tender.

CAVATAPPI WITH CHICKEN AND LEEKS

Time to make: 10 minutes
Time to cook: about 15 minutes

Serves 2

175 g (6 oz) dried cavatappi (corkscrews)

2 tablespoons sesame seeds

175 g (6 oz) leeks

175 g (6 oz) skinnned chicken breast fillet

2 tablespoons olive oil

1 teaspoon ginger purée

2 tablespoons chopped fresh coriander

salt and freshly ground black pepper to taste

coriander leaves to garnish

Whilst writing this book, Schwartz™ brought out jars of fresh ginger puréed with soya bean oil. I now keep one in my fridge at all times and add it to just about anything, as I am a committed ginger fan. Ginger isn't traditionally used in Italian cookery but it creates a vaguely oriental variation of a standard chicken and leek sauce which is full of flavour.

1 Bring a large saucepan of salted water to the boil, add the cavatappi and cook according to packet instructions until tender, which should take about 15 minutes.
2 Meanwhile put the sesame seeds in a frying pan and dry-fry for 2 minutes until toasted. Remove from heat and set aside. Trim and thinly slice the leeks and cut the chicken into 1 cm (½ in) slices.
3 When the cavatappi is half-cooked, heat the oil in a large frying pan. Add the ginger purée and chicken and cook for 5 minutes, stirring occasionally. Add the leeks and cook for 1 minute, stirring. Cover the pan with a tight-fitting lid and cook for 3 minutes.
4 Drain the cavatappi and immediately add it to the frying pan with the chopped coriander and sesame seeds. Season with salt and ground black pepper. Toss well to mix, garnish with coriander leaves and serve at once.

Cook's Tip
Watch the sesame seeds like a hawk, as they burn very quickly.

FARFALLE WITH TUNA AND CORIANDER

Time to make: 5 minutes
Time to cook: 10 to 15 minutes

Serves 2

175 g (6 oz) dried farfalle

4 anchovies in oil

1 small clove garlic

2 tablespoons fresh coriander leaves

5 tablespoons olive oil

½ teaspoon Dijon mustard

1 teaspoon red wine vinegar

pinch of dried chilli powder

198 g (7 oz) can tuna in oil

salt and freshly ground black pepper to taste

I've been making this pasta sauce for as long as I can remember. I started off making it with basil and then decided to experiment with coriander – and I've never looked back. Before I had a food processor I finely chopped the anchovies, garlic and coriander together before adding the other ingredients. It doesn't take very long, so don't be put off if you haven't got a processor.

1 Bring a large saucepan of salted water to the boil, add the farfalle and cook according to packet instructions until tender, which should take about 12 minutes.
2 Meanwhile drain the anchovies and put in a blender or food processor. Add the garlic, coriander, oil, mustard, red wine vinegar and chilli powder and process until smooth.
3 Drain the tuna, spoon into a mixing bowl and mash with a fork. Add the blended mixture and stir together. Season with ground black pepper.
4 Drain the farfalle and immediately return it to the pan. Add the sauce, tossing gently until the farfalle is well coated. Transfer to warmed serving plates and serve at once.

Cook's Tip
If you have any left over, this pasta dish is also delicious served cold as a salad.

FARFALLE WITH BEETROOT AND CRÈME FRAÎCHE

Time to make: 5 minutes
Time to cook: 10 to 15 minutes

Serves 4

350 g (12 oz) dried farfalle
175 g (6 oz) beetroot, cooked
200 ml (7 fl oz) carton crème fraîche
1 tablespoon creamed horseradish
2 tablespoons lemon juice
2 teaspoons balsamic vinegar
125 g (4 oz) feta cheese
snipped chives to garnish

This recipe was inspired by a dip that my friend Oona made at her nephew's christening. It may sound peculiar, but it certainly scores points for colour and taste and if you like beetroot, it's sure to become a favourite. Horseradish is a great combination with beetroot.

1   Bring a large saucepan of salted water to the boil, add the farfalle and cook according to packet instructions until tender, which should take about 12 minutes.
2   Meanwhile peel and roughly chop the beetroot. Put in a blender or food processor with the crème fraîche, horseradish, lemon juice and balsamic vinegar and process until smooth. Transfer to a saucepan, bring to the boil, then lower the heat and simmer, uncovered, for 8 minutes. Crumble the feta cheese into small pieces.
3   Drain the farfalle and immediately return it to the pan. Add the sauce and heat gently, tossing the mixture together until the farfalle is well coated. Transfer to warmed serving plates and sprinkle with the feta cheese and snipped chives. Serve at once, with a cucumber salad.

Cook's Tip
This sauce is best served fresh as the rich purple colour deteriorates to a rather nasty brown if it is left standing. As with avocados, you can prevent the colour change by adding a generous amount of lemon juice to the beetroot sauce, but it does make the sauce rather acidic – more like pickled beetroot.

Simply vegetables

More and more people are recognizing that the vegetarian diet – higher in fresh fruit, vegetables and starch and lower in saturated fat – is good for you. Pasta is the perfect medium for vegetarian sauces and with the emphasis here on Mediterranean flavours you won't even notice that you are eating 'vegetarian'.

CONCHIGLIE WITH PUMPKIN AND CORIANDER

Time to make: 5 minutes
Time to cook: 15 to 20 minutes

Serves 4

500 g (1 lb) wedge of pumpkin

5 cm (2 in) piece fresh root ginger

2 cloves garlic

125 g (4 oz) butter

142 ml (5 fl oz) carton double cream

1 tablespoon demerara sugar

1 tablespoon lemon juice

350 g (12 oz) dried conchiglie

salt and freshly ground black pepper to taste

6 tablespoons chopped fresh coriander

coriander leaves to garnish

This recipe was inspired by a vegetable dish served at The Wilds restaurant in Fulham. When I was working there I used to keep nipping down to the kitchen to pinch a spoonful as it tasted so good. Since then I've developed this recipe, as the creaminess of the pumpkin together with the flavour of ginger and coriander work really well as a pasta sauce. I've used conchiglie as the large shells hold the sauce well, but you could also use penne.

1   Using a sharp knife, peel the skin from the pumpkin and discard the seeds. Grate the flesh, using a food processor fitted with a grating attachment or by hand. Peel and finely chop the ginger and crush the garlic .
2   Meanwhile melt the butter in a large heavy-based frying pan, add the ginger and garlic and cook for 2 minutes. Add the pumpkin flesh, cover and simmer gently for 15 minutes, stirring occasionally, until the pumpkin is soft and creamy.
3   Stir in the cream, demerara sugar and lemon juice. Cook over low heat for 2 minutes, stirring constantly to make a smooth, creamy sauce.
4   Meanwhile bring a large saucepan of salted water to the boil, add the conchiglie and cook according to packet instructions until just tender, which should take 10 to 12 minutes.
5   Drain the conchiglie and immediately stir it into the sauce. Season with salt and ground black pepper, add the chopped coriander and toss until all the shells are well coated with the sauce. Serve at once, garnished with coriander leaves.

Cook's Tip
I've added demerara sugar to sweeten the sauce, but use granulated or caster if you don't have demerara to hand. If pumpkin is out of season, use butternut squash instead.

Stirring the conchiglie into the sauce

SPAGHETTI WITH STIR-FRIED VEGETABLES

Time to make: 15 minutes
Time to cook: 5 to 10 minutes

Serves 4

1 large red pepper

1 large yellow pepper

1 clove garlic

1 bunch of spring onions

2.5 cm (1 in) piece fresh root ginger

125 g (4 oz) mange tout

227 g (8 oz) can sliced bamboo shoots

1 teaspoon cornflour

2 tablespoons soy sauce

2 tablespoons dry sherry

300 g (10 oz) dried quick-cook spaghetti

1 teaspoon sesame oil

2 teaspoons sunflower oil

125 g (4 oz) broccoli florets

I wrote this recipe years ago for a feature in Woman magazine. It was originally cooked with lambs' liver, as the whole purpose of the feature was to encourage children to eat liver – by way of disguising it. However, since this chapter is vegetarian, I have left out the liver and cooked it purely with vegetables. I have used spaghetti but tagliatelle works just as well and I have also made it with egg noodles.

1 Cut the peppers into quarters, remove the core and seeds, then cut the flesh widthways into thin strips. Crush the garlic. Slice the spring onions into 2.5 cm (1 in) pieces. Peel and grate the ginger. Top and tail the mange tout and cut in half widthways. Drain the bamboo shoots.
2 Blend the cornflour with 2 tablespoons water in a small jug. Stir in the soy sauce and sherry.
3 Bring a large saucepan of salted water to the boil, add the spaghetti and cook according to packet instructions until tender, which should take about 5 minutes.
4 Meanwhile heat the sesame and sunflower oils in a wok or large frying pan. Add the peppers, garlic, spring onions, ginger and broccoli florets and stir-fry for 3 minutes until the vegetables begin to soften. Add the mange tout and bamboo shoots and stir-fry for a further 2 minutes.
5 Stir in the cornflour mixture and cook, stirring constantly, for 2 minutes until thickened.
6 Drain the spaghetti and immediately return it to the pan. Add the vegetables and heat gently, tossing the mixture together until well mixed. Serve at once with extra soy sauce.

Cook's Tips
It's worth buying quick-cook spaghetti for this dish, as it takes the same amount of time to cook as the stir-fried vegetables. If you use ordinary spaghetti, put it on to boil after you have prepared the vegetables and start stir-frying 5 minutes before the spaghetti is cooked.
Cut the vegetables into similar size pieces so that they cook evenly.

TAGLIARINI WITH DOLCELATTE AND SPINACH

Time to make: 10 minutes
Time to cook: about 10 minutes

Serves 4

1 large Spanish onion
2 cloves garlic
350 g (12 oz) young leaf spinach or chopped frozen spinach, thawed
250 g (8 oz) dolcelatte
25 g (1 oz) butter
5 tablespoons milk
400 g (14 oz) fresh mixed tagliarini
salt and freshly ground black pepper to taste
pinch of freshly grated nutmeg

Spinach and blue cheese have to be one of my favourite combinations and this chapter would not be complete without a sauce using these two ingredients. I have used tagliarini, a fine long pasta which marries well with creamy sauces – it also comes as a mix of plain, spinach and tomato which cheer up the dreary colour of wilted spinach. Alternatively, you could use tagliatelle, linguini or spaghetti. If you like a stronger sauce, use gorgonzola instead of dolcelatte. On the other hand, if you're not a fan of blue cheese, feta works equally well.

1   Finely chop the onion and garlic. If using fresh spinach, remove any large stalks. Put the spinach in a non-stick saucepan and cook for 3 minutes, stirring, until wilted. Drain well in a sieve, pressing out any excess water.
2   Crumble the dolcelatta into small pieces. Melt the butter in a large frying pan, add the onion and garlic and cook for 4 minutes until softened. Add the milk and dolcelatta and cook over a low heat, stirring until melted to a creamy sauce.
3   Meanwhile bring a large saucepan of salted water to the boil, add the tagliarini and cook according to packet instructions until tender, which should take about 3 minutes.
4   Add the spinach to the sauce and season with ground black pepper and nutmeg. Drain the tagliarini, stir it into the sauce and toss until well coated. Serve at once.

Cook's Tip
Drain the cooked spinach thoroughly by pressing it against the sieve with the back of a wooden spoon.

COUSCOUS WITH MOROCCAN SPICED VEGETABLES

Time to make: 30 minutes
Time to cook: 30 minutes

Serves 4

250 g (8 oz) couscous

1 large aubergine, about 250 g (8 oz)

175 g (6 oz) courgettes

175 g (6 oz) carrots

1 large onion

2 cloves garlic

2 tablespoons olive oil

1 teaspoon mild chilli powder

1 teaspoon ground ginger

1 teaspoon ground cinnamon

3 teaspoons ground cumin

170 g (6 oz) can chick peas

397 g (14 oz) can chopped tomatoes

2 tablespoons tomato purée

300 ml (10 fl oz) vegetable stock

salt and freshly ground black pepper to taste

4 tablespoons Greek-style yogurt

1 tablespoon lemon juice

1 tablespoon chopped fresh parsley to serve

flat-leaf parsley sprigs to garnish

I've never thought that pasta should be confined to sauces with a purely Italian influence – in fact, I think that flavours from all over the Mediterranean work well, particularly couscous. Couscous is the name given to both the national dish of Morocco and the durum wheat pasta granules from which it is made. The granules are steamed over the saucepan containing the vegetables, absorbing all the flavours of the vegetables and spices as it cooks in the steam.

1 Put the couscous in a bowl and cover with water according to packet instructions. Cut the aubergine and courgettes into 1 cm (½ in) dice. Roughly chop the carrots, finely chop the onion and crush the garlic.
2 Heat the oil in a large frying pan over low heat. Add the carrot, onion, garlic, chilli powder, ground ginger and cinnamon and 2 teaspoons of the ground cumin. Cook over low heat for 5 minutes, stirring occasionally, until the vegetables soften.
3 Meanwhile drain and fork the couscous to break up any lumps and spread in a steamer, metal sieve or colander lined with muslin.
4 Drain and rinse the chick peas and add to the pan with the aubergine, courgette, tomatoes and tomato purée. Pour in the stock, bring to the boil, then lower the heat and simmer uncovered for 10 minutes until the sauce is well reduced. Put the couscous container over the pan of vegetables, cover and simmer for 15 minutes. Season with salt and ground black pepper.
5 Meanwhile spoon the yogurt into a small mixing bowl. Stir in the lemon juice, remaining ground cumin and seasoning.
6 Transfer the couscous to warmed serving plates and fork through. Spoon the vegetables and cooking juices over the couscous and top with a spoonful of the yogurt mixture. Sprinkle with chopped parsley and garnish with a parsley sprig to serve.

Cook's Tip
Couscous varies tremendously from brand to brand, so be sure to check the cooking instructions on the packet before you start. It is possible to buy quick-cook which will only need steaming over the vegetables for 5 to 10 minutes.

ORECCHIETTE WITH AUBERGINE AND SUN-DRIED TOMATOES

Time to make: 45 minutes
Time to cook: about 15 minutes

Serves 2

1 small aubergine
salt and freshly ground black pepper to taste
2 sun-dried tomatoes in oil
125 g (4 oz) Bavarian smoked cheese
1 egg yolk
6 tablespoons double cream
250 g (8 oz) dried orecchiette
2 tablespoons olive oil
4 tablespoons dry white wine

Whilst writing this book, I went to Bertorelli's in Covent Garden for lunch and had the most stunning risotto made with aubergine, sun-dried tomatoes and Bavarian smoked cheese. The creaminess of the rice worked really well with the stringiness of the cheese and the texture of the aubergine. The recipe below is based on the flavours of the risotto but cooked with orecchiette or 'little ears'.

1 Cut the aubergine into 1 cm (½ in) dice, toss in 2 teaspoons salt and spoon into a colander. Leave for 30 minutes to allow some of the bitter juices to drain out. Rinse in cold water and squeeze dry on absorbent kitchen paper.

2 Meanwhile drain the sun-dried tomatoes on absorbent kitchen paper, then chop roughly. Remove the rind from the cheese, then cut into small dice. Put the egg yolk in a bowl and stir in the cream and cheese. Season with salt and ground black pepper. Set aside.

3 Just before you rinse the aubergine, bring a large saucepan of salted water to the boil, add the orecchiette and cook according to packet instructions until tender, which should take about 14 minutes.

4 Meanwhile heat the oil in a large saucepan, add the aubergine and cook over high heat for 5 minutes, stirring occasionally, until golden brown. Stir in the wine and sun-dried tomatoes, bring to the boil, then lower the heat and simmer until the wine has reduced by half.

5 Drain the orecchiette and immediately return it to the pan. Add the aubergine and the egg mixture. Return to the heat and simmer gently for 2 minutes, stirring constantly, until the sauce thickens and the cheese begins to melt. Check seasoning and serve at once.

FUSILLI WITH OYSTER MUSHROOMS AND TOMATOES

Time to make: 25 minutes
Time to cook: about 15 minutes

Serves 4

25 g (1 oz) dried porcini mushrooms

2 cloves garlic

350 g (12 oz) oyster mushrooms

3 tablespoons olive oil

2 tablespoons chopped fresh parsley

350 g (12 oz) dried fusilli

227 g (8 oz) can chopped tomatoes

salt and freshly ground black pepper to taste

25 g (1 oz) butter

6 tablespoons freshly grated Parmesan cheese

Porcini mushrooms add a wonderful strong woodland mushroom flavour to this pasta sauce. Fresh porcini mushrooms are hard to find, but dried varieties are available in good delicatessens and some supermarkets. They're sold in clear plastic packets and look like small pieces of dried wood. They make a great store-cupboard ingredient as they last forever wrapped in non-pvc clear film. Beware of the cheaper varieties which are mostly stems.

1   Put the porcini in a bowl, add 300 ml (10 fl oz) warm water and leave to soak for 20 minutes. Meanwhile crush the garlic and slice the oyster mushrooms.

2   Heat the oil in a large frying pan, add the garlic and sauté for 3 minutes until it begins to change colour, then stir in 1 tablespoon of the parsley. Set aside.

3   Remove the porcini from the water with a slotted spoon and squeeze out any excess water back into the bowl. Reserve the soaking water. Roughly chop the porcini.

4   Bring a large saucepan of salted water to the boil, add the fusilli and cook according to packet instructions until tender, which should take about 12 minutes.

5   Meanwhile add the porcini and soaking water to the garlic and parsley and cook uncovered until all the water has evaporated.

6   Add the oyster mushrooms to the pan and cook for 5 minutes until any water they release has evaporated. Add the tomatoes and season with salt and ground black pepper. Cook for 5 minutes until the tomatoes have reduced and separated from the oil. Check seasoning.

7   Drain the fusilli and immediately return it to the pan. Add the sauce, butter and Parmesan cheese and toss together until the fusilli is well coated. Sprinkle with the remaining parsley and serve at once.

RAVIOLI WITH ROASTED VEGETABLE VINAIGRETTE

Time to make: 25 minutes, plus
  standing time
Time to cook: 10 to 15 minutes

Serves 4

1 large yellow pepper

1 large red pepper

1 bulb fennel

2 cloves garlic

150 ml (5 fl oz) olive oil

salt and freshly ground black pepper to taste

2 tablespoons pine nuts

6 tablespoons balsamic vinegar

550 g (1 lb 2 oz) fresh pecorino and basil ravioli or other cheese-based fresh filled pasta

2 tablespoons chopped fresh basil

purple basil leaves to garnish

A perfect dish to take on a picnic, this recipe can be adapted to serve with any of the huge selection of fresh ravioli now available in supermarkets.

1   Halve, core and seed the yellow and red peppers, then cut into quarters. Trim any fronds from the fennel and reserve. Cut the fennel into quarters. Preheat the grill to high.

2   Put the peppers, fennel and unpeeled garlic cloves on a non-stick baking sheet and brush with a little of the olive oil. Season with salt and ground black pepper. Grill for about 5 minutes, turning once, until lightly charred and blistered. Put the peppers and garlic in a plastic bag for 2 minutes to loosen skin. Set fennel aside to cool .

3   Sprinkle the pine nuts onto the baking sheet and grill for 1 to 2 minutes, turning occasionally, until golden. Set aside.

4   Pour the remaining olive oil into a screw-top jar. Add the balsamic vinegar, season with salt and ground black pepper and shake until well blended. Set aside.

5   Peel and roughly chop the garlic and peel the skin from the peppers. Finely chop half of the peppers and fennel and cut the rest into 1 cm (½ in) slices. Put the chopped pepper and fennel in a large mixing bowl. Add the garlic and the vinaigrette mixture and stir well to mix.

6   Bring a large saucepan of salted water to the boil, add the ravioli and cook according to packet instructions until tender, which should take about 4 minutes. Drain and rinse carefully in cold water.

7   Add the ravioli to the chopped vegetables. Add the sliced roasted pepper and fennel and chopped basil and toss together. Leave to stand for at least 1 hour to allow the flavours to combine.

8   Chop reserved fennel fronds. Transfer the ravioli to serving plates, sprinkle with the fronds and pine nuts and garnish with basil leaves.

Cook's Tip
This salad is best served at room temperature, so if made in advance and stored in the fridge, remove an hour before serving.

FARFALLE WITH COURGETTE, PECORINO AND MINT

Time to make: 10 minutes
Time to cook: 20 to 25 minutes

Serves 4

1 onion

2 cloves garlic

500 g (1 lb) courgettes

4 tablespoons olive oil

500 g (1 lb) dried farfalle

1 tablespoon chopped fresh parsley

4 tablespoons shredded basil

1 teaspoon finely chopped fresh mint

salt and freshly ground black pepper to taste

4 tablespoons freshly grated pecorino cheese

I must admit that courgette served as a vegetable on its own is not a favourite of mine, as I find it rather dreary. Add some onion, garlic, mint and pecorino cheese, however, and it comes into its own. Pecorino is a hard yellow cheese made from sheeps' milk. It's sharper than Parmesan and a little more expensive, but a little goes a long way and its tart flavour makes all the difference in this recipe.

1   Halve and thinly slice the onion. Crush the garlic. Cut the courgettes into matchstick size pieces.
2   Heat the oil in a large heavy-based frying pan. Add the onion and cook over low heat for 10 minutes, stirring occasionally, until soft.
3   Meanwhile bring a large saucepan of salted water to the boil, add the farfalle and cook according to packet instructions until tender, which should take about 12 minutes.
4   Add the garlic to the frying pan, increase the heat and cook for 2 minutes until the garlic begins to change colour. Add the parsley and courgettes and stir well. Cook for 5 to 10 minutes, stirring occasionally, until the courgettes are lightly browned and tender. Stir in the basil and mint and season with salt and ground black pepper.
5   Drain the farfalle and immediately return it to the pan. Add the courgette mixture and the pecorino and heat gently, tossing together until the farfalle is well coated. Serve at once.

Cook's Tip
Some major supermarkets now stock purple basil. It has a hint of mint about it and works brilliantly in this dish. Use just over 4 tablespoons in place of the mint and basil in the recipe.

FRESH PENNE WITH ROASTED PEPPERS

Time to make: 20 minutes
Time to cook: about 30 minutes

Serves 4

2 large green peppers
2 large red peppers
2 large yellow peppers
4 tablespoons pine nuts
550 g (1 lb 2 oz) fresh penne
50 g (2 oz) fresh basil leaves
2 cloves garlic
150 ml (5 fl oz) olive oil
salt and freshly ground black pepper to taste
25 g (1 oz) freshly grated Parmesan cheese
2 tablespoons shredded fresh basil to garnish

Photographed on page 3

Sweet grilled peppers together with fresh homemade pesto complement each other really well in this dish. I've used red, green and yellow peppers as it's cheaper to buy the packs of mixed peppers. If you prefer you can use six of the same colour – the more yellow peppers you use, the sweeter the sauce.

1 Set the oven to 190C, 375F, Gas 5. Put the peppers on a baking sheet and bake for 25 minutes, turning once.
2 Meanwhile preheat the grill to high. Sprinkle the pine nuts into the grill pan and grill for 1 to 2 minutes, turning every 30 seconds, until golden. Leave to cool.
3 Put the peppers in a plastic bag for about 5 minutes to loosen the skins, then peel, halve, core, seed and slice into 1 cm (½ in) strips.
4 Bring a large saucepan of salted water to the boil, add the penne and cook according to packet instructions until just tender, which should take about 5 minutes.
5 Meanwhile put 2 tablespoons of the pine nuts, the basil leaves, garlic and oil in a blender or food processor and process until smooth. Season with salt and ground black pepper.
6 Drain the penne and immediately return it to pan. Add the prepared pesto, peppers and 3 tablespoons water. Cook for 2 minutes until the peppers are heated through.
7 Sprinkle with the Parmesan cheese, then transfer to warmed serving plates. Garnish with the basil and remaining pine nuts and serve at once.

Cook's Tip
Unless you have asbestos hands, or don't mind waiting until the peppers are cold, I find it easier to peel and seed the peppers wearing a clean pair of rubber gloves – that way you don't burn your fingers.

FIORELLI WITH ROASTED VEGETABLES AND TAPENADE

Time to make: 10 minutes
Time to cook: 40 minutes

Serves 4

1 large red pepper

2 small red onions

1 bulb fennel

2 courgettes

250 g (8 oz) cherry tomatoes

2 tablespoons extra-virgin olive oil

1 tablespoon chopped fresh marjoram, basil or thyme

salt and freshly ground black pepper to taste

350 g (12 oz) dried fiorelli

mixed fresh herbs to garnish, optional

4 tablespoons freshly grated Parmesan cheese to serve

Tapenade

250 g (8 oz) pitted black olives

1 tablespoon capers

1 fat clove garlic

1 teaspoon lemon juice

5 tablespoons extra-virgin olive oil

Roasted vegetables must be one of the tastiest and most colourful toppings for pasta and are very easy to prepare. Here I've tossed the pasta in tapenade, a rich olive paste, before piling it high with the vegetables. If you're feeling particularly lazy, you can buy ready-made tapenade from delicatessens and larger supermarkets. I have used fiorelli, which look like little frilled trumpets – I have also seen them called campanelle. You could also use conchiglie.

1   Set the oven to 240C, 475F, Gas 9. Halve, core and seed the pepper and cut into 2.5 cm (1 in) squares. Cut the onions and fennel into wedges, leaving the roots intact. Roughly chop the courgettes into chunks.

2   Arrange the peppers, onions, fennel, courgettes and tomatoes in a roasting tin. Drizzle over the oil and sprinkle with the marjoram, basil or thyme. Toss the vegetables to coat in the oil and season with salt and ground black pepper. Cook on the top shelf of the oven for 40 minutes, stirring occasionally, until the vegetables begin to blacken at the edges.

3   Meanwhile make the tapenade. Put the olives, capers, garlic, lemon juice and oil in a blender or food processor and process to a paste .

4   Bring a large saucepan of salted water to the boil, add the fiorelli and cook according to packet instructions until just tender, which should take 10 to 12 minutes.

5   Drain the fiorelli thoroughly. Add the tapenade to the pasta pan and heat gently for a few seconds. Return the fiorelli to the pan and toss to mix. Transfer to warmed serving plates and top with the roasted vegetables. Garnish with herbs if wished and serve with the Parmesan cheese.

VEGETARIAN LASAGNE

Time to make: 50 minutes
Time to cook: 1 to 1¼ hours

Serves 6

250 g (8 oz) aubergines

500 g (1 lb) courgettes

salt and freshly ground black pepper to taste

1 onion

1 clove garlic

397 g (14 oz) can chopped tomatoes

1 small red pepper

1 small green pepper

1 small yellow pepper

350 g (12 oz) even-size small tomatoes

6 tablespoons olive oil

1 tablespoon tomato purée

1 tablespoon chopped fresh oregano

125 g (4 oz) easy-cook lasagne verdi

1 teaspoon chopped fresh thyme

Cheese Sauce

250 g (8 oz) Cheddar cheese

300 ml (10 fl oz) milk

3 tablespoons plain flour

1 teaspoon English mustard

This substantial dish, made with rich ratatouille and all-in-one cheese sauce, is an excellent choice if you suddenly have to cook for large numbers and you're not sure if any of them are vegetarian.

1   Slice the aubergines and half of the courgettes. Layer in a colander or sieve, sprinkling each layer with a generous amount of salt. Leave to stand for 30 minutes, then rinse in cold water and pat dry with absorbent kitchen paper.
2   Meanwhile chop the onion and crush the garlic. Drain the canned tomatoes and discard the juice. Halve, core, seed and slice the peppers. Thinly slice the fresh tomatoes.
3   Heat 4 tablespoons of the oil in a large saucepan, add the onion and garlic and cook for 10 minutes until soft and golden.
4   Add the aubergine and courgette and cook, stirring occasionally, for 5 minutes until beginning to brown. Add end slices only of the fresh tomato, the canned tomatoes, tomato purée, peppers, oregano and seasoning. Bring to the boil, then lower the heat, cover and simmer for 15 minutes.
5   To make the cheese sauce: grate the Cheddar cheese. Pour the milk into a large saucepan and add the flour. Bring to the boil, whisking constantly until the mixture begins to thicken. Remove from heat and add the cheese and mustard. Return to heat and cook for 2 minutes, stirring until the cheese has melted. Remove from heat and season with salt and ground black pepper.
6   Spoon half of the tomato sauce into a 2 litre (3½ pint) ovenproof dish. Cover with half of the lasagne sheets in a single layer. Sprinkle with 1 teaspoon water. Spoon over half of the cheese sauce. Repeat the layers once more, finishing with cheese sauce.
7   Set the oven to 190C, 375F, Gas 5. Thinly slice the remaining courgettes. Arrange the reserved tomato slices and courgettes overlapping on the sauce. Drizzle over the remaining oil and sprinkle with the thyme.
8   Put the dish on a baking sheet and bake in the centre of the oven for 30 to 40 minutes until the lasagne is soft and the cheese is bubbling. Leave to stand for 2 minutes before serving.

RIGATONI WITH THREE CHEESES

Time to make: 5 minutes
Time to cook: about 15 minutes

Serves 8

2 onions

2 cloves garlic

3 tablespoons extra-virgin olive oil

250 g (8 oz) goats' cheese

250 g (8 oz) gruyère cheese

300 ml (10 fl oz) dry white wine

125 g (4 oz) freshly grated Parmesan cheese

4 tablespoons chopped fresh parsley

salt and freshly ground black pepper to taste

1.25 kg (2 lb 4 oz) fresh rigatoni

parsley sprigs to garnish

Half the fun of having friends round for supper is having time to sit down with them for a glass of wine and a chat and not having to spend ages in the kitchen preparing food. This three-cheese pasta recipe takes about 10 minutes to make and is brilliant as a last-minute dish, particularly if you're not one for preparing food in advance. It is not, however, a recipe for anyone watching their weight or fat intake, although served with a green salad such as rocket and finished with fresh fruit, the meal will be reasonably balanced as well as delicious.

1 Bring one very large pan or two large pans of salted water to the boil. Finely chop the onions and crush the garlic.
2 Heat the oil in a large saucepan, add the onion and garlic and cook over low heat for 5 minutes, stirring occasionally, until the onions have softened.
3 Meanwhile cut the rind from the goats' cheese and gruyère and discard. Roughly chop the cheeses into small dice.
4 Add the wine to the onion mixture. Bring to the boil, then lower the heat and simmer for 3 minutes until reduced by half. Add the goats' cheese, gruyère, grated Parmesan and chopped parsley. Bring almost to the boil, then lower the heat and simmer gently for 5 to 6 minutes until all the cheese has melted. Season with salt and ground black pepper.
5 Meanwhile add the rigatoni to the pan(s) of boiling water and cook according to packet instructions until tender, which should take about 5 minutes.
6 Drain the rigatoni and immediately return it to the pan(s). Add the sauce and toss until the rigatoni is well coated. Transfer to warmed serving plates and garnish with parsley sprigs. Serve at once.

Cook's Tip
Rigatoni are the short ridged hollow tubes. They're great for this sauce as the cheese melts into the tubes which makes it easy to eat. You could also use conchiglie rigate (ridged shells) or penne (quills).

The classics

No self-respecting Italian restaurant would be without a few of the classics on its menu, and neither should any useful pasta book! Here you will find Lasagne, Cannelloni and Spaghetti alla Carbonara. But although I have tested more than seventy recipes for this book, I have to admit to going back to the old faithful recipe, based on a classic, time and time again – my Mum's Spaghetti Bolognaise!

SPAGHETTI ALLE VONGOLE

Time to make: 20 minutes
Time to cook: about 15 minutes

Serves 4

500 g (1 lb) baby clams in shells

2 cloves garlic

4 tablespoons extra-virgin olive oil

pinch of crushed chillies

150 ml (5 fl oz) dry white wine

2 tablespoons chopped fresh parsley

350 g (12 oz) dried spaghetti

25 g (1 oz) butter

This classic recipe takes its name from the Italian word *vongola* or clam. There are many versions around, some with tomato and some without, some with mussels and some without. I prefer mine simple – no tomato and no mussels – just clams, garlic, wine and parsley, with loads of bread to mop up the sauce.

1 Wash the clams in cold water and scrub the shells with a small nailbrush. Leave to soak in cold water for at least 10 minutes. Crush the garlic.
2 Heat the oil in a pan large enough to hold the spaghetti later. Add the garlic and chillies and cook over low heat for 2 minutes until the garlic is lightly browned.
3 Rinse the clams in fresh cold water and discard any which don't close when they are lightly tapped. Add to the pan with the wine and parsley . Bring to the boil and cook, stirring occasionally, until the wine has evaporated. Cover with a tight-fitting lid and cook for 3 minutes to steam open the clams. Discard any clams which have not opened.
4 Meanwhile bring a large saucepan of salted water to the boil, add the spaghetti and cook according to packet instructions until almost tender, which should take about 12 minutes. Drain thoroughly and return it to the pan.
5 Add the clam sauce and butter and heat gently, tossing lightly, until the spaghetti is cooked. Serve at once.

Adding the clams and butter to the spaghetti

FETTUCINE ALL'ALFREDO

Time to make: 5 minutes
Time to cook: 15 minutes

Serves 4 to 6

1 tablespoon olive oil

40 g (1½ oz) butter

300 ml (10 fl oz) double cream

1 teaspoon freshly grated nutmeg

salt and freshly ground black pepper to taste

550 g (1 lb 2 oz) fresh fettucine

75 g (3 oz) freshly grated Parmesan cheese

Not for the weak of heart, this classic pasta dish from Rome is simply pasta tossed in cream and butter. I find it best served with a vinegar-laden dressed salad as the acidity of the dressing complements the richness of the sauce. If this recipe weren't in this chapter, it would be in the quick and easy chapter as it takes minutes to make.

1   Bring a large saucepan of salted water to the boil, add the oil and keep simmering. Put the butter and cream in a small heavy-based saucepan. Bring to the boil, stirring frequently, then lower the heat and simmer very gently for 15 minutes, stirring occasionally, until the cream has reduced by half. Add the nutmeg and season with salt and plenty of ground black pepper.
2   Add the fettucine to the pan of simmering water and cook according to packet instructions until nearly tender, which should take about 4 minutes.
3   Drain the fettucine and immediately return it to the pan. Add the cream sauce and Parmesan, tossing together until the fettucine is well coated. Check seasoning and serve at once.

Cook's Tip
Take great care when heating the cream, otherwise it will burn. Bring it slowly just to boiling point, then simmer over very low heat.

CANNELLONI

Time to make: 1 hour
Time to cook: about 40 minutes,
  plus standing time

Serves 4

3 shallots

1 onion

2 cloves garlic

125 g (4 oz) mozzarella cheese

75 g (3 oz) butter

150 g (6 oz) lean minced beef

salt and freshly ground black
pepper to taste

2 tablespoons olive oil

450 ml (15 fl oz) passata

12 cannelloni tubes

300 ml (10 fl oz) milk

6 tablespoons plain flour

pinch of freshly grated nutmeg

1 egg yolk

250 g (8 oz) ricotta cheese

150 g (5 oz) freshly grated
Parmesan cheese

Preparing cannelloni is time-consuming but quite simple and
worth the effort. If you can't find cannelloni tubes use lasagne
sheets and roll them up like a Swiss roll. You might also like to try
filling combinations of chicken and mozzarella, veal and spinach,
chicken and tarragon, as well as the spinach and ricotta classic.

1   Finely chop the shallots and onion, keeping them separate.
Crush the garlic. Finely chop the mozzarella into small dice.
2   Melt 25 g (1 oz) of the butter in a saucepan. Add the shallots
and cook for 5 minutes until softened. Add the minced beef and
cook, crumbling with a wooden spoon, until browned. Season
with salt and ground black pepper. Remove the meat and shallots
with a slotted spoon and put in a mixing bowl. Leave to cool.
3   Heat the oil in a saucepan, add the onion and garlic and cook
for 5 minutes, until softened. Stir in the passata and season with
salt and ground black pepper. Cover and simmer gently for 5
minutes. Remove from heat and set aside.
4   Bring a large saucepan of salted water to the boil, add the
cannelloni and cook according to packet instructions until tender,
which should take about 7 minutes. Drain on a clean tea-towel.
5   Meanwhile pour the milk into a saucepan, add the remaining
butter and the flour and bring to the boil, whisking constantly
until the sauce thickens. Season with salt and ground black
pepper. Remove from heat and cover the surface with non-pvc
clear film to prevent a skin forming.
6   Set the oven to 180C, 350F, Gas 4. When the meat mixture is
cool, add the mozzarella, nutmeg, egg yolk, ricotta cheese and
100 g (4 oz) of the Parmesan cheese. Mix well with a fork to a
piping consistency; if the mixture is too thick, add 2 to 3
tablespoons of the prepared white sauce. Spoon into a large piping
bag fitted with a plain nozzle and use to fill each cannelloni tube.
7   Pour the tomato sauce into a 25 x 20 cm (10 x 8 in) ovenproof
dish. Arrange the cannelloni in a single layer on top. Pour over
the white sauce and sprinkle with the remaining Parmesan cheese.
Bake on the top shelf of the oven for 15 to 20 minutes until a
golden crust forms on the top. Leave for 10 minutes before serving.

FETTUCINE PRIMAVERA

Time to make: 20 minutes
Time to cook: about 20 minutes

Serves 4

1 onion
125 g (4 oz) mange tout
175 g (6 oz) fine asparagus, optional
250 g (8 oz) baby carrots
250 g (8 oz) courgettes
50 g (2 oz) butter
400 g (14 oz) fresh paglia e fieno (green and yellow fettucine)
284 ml (10 fl oz) carton double cream
4 tablespoons freshly grated Parmesan cheese
2 tablespoons snipped fresh chives
2 tablespoons chopped fresh chervil
salt and freshly ground black pepper to taste
fresh chervil sprigs and chives to garnish

Another of the Italian classics – ribbon pasta with spring vegetables. Traditionally this is served as a dish in its own right, but I tend to serve it as an accompaniment to grilled chicken or salmon – it makes a welcome change to potatoes and vegetables or bread and salad.

1   Finely chop the onion. Top and tail the mange tout. Halve the asparagus spears if using. If the carrots are very small simply scrape them and leave whole, otherwise peel them and cut into matchstick size pieces. Slice the courgettes.
2   Melt the butter in a large frying pan. Add the onion, cover and cook over low heat for 5 minutes without browning. Stir in the courgettes and carrots and cook uncovered for a further 7 minutes until the vegetables are beginning to colour.
3   Add the mange tout and asparagus, if using, stir gently and cook for 3 minutes.
4   Meanwhile bring a large saucepan of salted water to the boil, add the pasta and cook according to packet instructions until tender, which should take about 4 minutes.
5   Stir the cream into the vegetables and bring to the boil. Boil gently until the cream has reduced by about one-third. Add the Parmesan cheese, snipped chives and chopped chervil. Cook for 1 minute, then season with salt and ground black pepper.
6   Drain the pasta thoroughly and immediately return it to the pan. Add the vegetable mixture and toss together until well mixed. Garnish with chervil and chives and serve at once.

Cook's Tip
Ring the changes by using pappardelle (ribbons) or tagliatelle instead of fettucine.

LASAGNE

Time to make: 15 minutes, plus
    standing time
Time to cook: about 45 minutes

Serves 4 to 6

1 small carrot

1 small onion

1 stick celery

900 ml (30 fl oz) milk

5 peppercorns

**175 g (6 oz) dried lasagne verdi
(9 sheets)**

1 tablespoon oil

75 g (3 oz) butter

40 g (1½ oz) plain flour

**50 g (2 oz) freshly grated
Parmesan cheese**

**salt and freshly ground black
pepper to taste**

**¼ teaspoon freshly grated
nutmeg**

**1 quantity bolognaise sauce
(see page 61)**

To me this is one of the all-time classics and a safe bet when entertaining. I have never found a convenience version that is anything like the real thing and although it's not a dish you can knock up in an instant, once it's made you can just sling it in the oven and it simply cooks itself with no last-minute fuss . The classic version is thin layers of green pasta layered with thick ragu Bolognese and creamy béchamel sauce. I add Parmesan cheese and a little freshly grated nutmeg to the sauce.

1 Butter the base and sides of an 18 x 23 cm (7 x 9 in) lasagne dish. Roughly chop the carrot and onion. Slice the celery. Pour the milk into a large saucepan and add the carrot, onion, celery and peppercorns. Bring to the boil, then remove from heat and leave to stand for 30 minutes.
2 Bring a large saucepan of salted water to the boil, add the lasagne sheets and oil and cook according to packet instructions until tender, which should take about 8 minutes. Plunge into a bowl of cold water, then drain on absorbent kitchen paper.
3 Strain the milk through a sieve into a large mixing bowl. Discard the vegetables. Melt the butter in the same saucepan, then stir in the flour. Cook, stirring, for 2 minutes.
4 Remove from heat and add the strained milk all at once. Whisk well with a balloon whisk until the sauce is creamy. Return to heat and simmer for 2 minutes. Stir in 25 g (1 oz) of the Parmesan cheese and season with salt, ground black pepper and nutmeg.
5 Set the oven to 180C, 350F, Gas 4. Spoon one-third of the bolognaise sauce into the prepared dish . Cover with 3 sheets of lasagne and spread with one-third of the cheese sauce, making sure the sauce goes right to the edges of the dish. Repeat the process twice more, finishing with a layer of cheese sauce covering the top.
6 Sprinkle with the remaining Parmesan cheese. Place on a baking sheet and bake in the centre of the oven for 30 to 35 minutes until brown and bubbling. Serve with a crisp green salad.

SPAGHETTI ALLA CARBONARA

Time to make: 10 minutes
Time to cook: about 15 minutes

Serves 4

400 g (14 oz) dried spaghetti

125 g (4 oz) smoked sliced pancetta (see Cook's Tip)

25 g (1 oz) butter

6 tablespoons dry white wine

3 eggs

40 g (1½ oz) freshly grated Parmesan cheese

40 g (1½ oz) freshly grated pecorino cheese

2 tablespoons chopped fresh parsley

salt and freshly ground black pepper to taste

Carbonara is one of those dishes I choose when my eyes are bigger than my belly, which is OK as long as I'm wearing clothes with an elasticated waist! Many of the recipes I've seen for this dish use cream but traditionally it is made simply with eggs and cheese, with the heat of the spaghetti setting the eggs and melting the cheese to a creamy texture. If you're not fond of the idea of slightly undercooked eggs, choose another dish, as overcooking the eggs doesn't do this dish the justice it deserves.

1 Bring a large saucepan of salted water to the boil, add the spaghetti and cook according to packet instructions until tender, which should take about 15 minutes.
2 Meanwhile cut the pancetta into thin strips. Melt the butter in a frying pan, add the pancetta and cook for 3 minutes until it is well browned but not crisp. Pour in the wine and boil gently until it has reduced by half.
3 In a mixing bowl large enough to hold the cooked spaghetti, lightly beat the eggs with the Parmesan, pecorino and parsley. Season with a pinch of salt and several grindings of black pepper.
4 Drain the spaghetti and immediately add it to the bowl with the hot pancetta. Toss well to cook the eggs until they are creamy. Serve at once.

Cook's Tip
Pancetta is available from all good delicatessens, but if you can't get it, use smoked bacon instead. You will need about 50 g (2 oz) more than the pancetta to give sufficient flavour.

TORTELLINI ALLA BOSCAIOLA

Time to make: 15 minutes
Time to cook: about 15 minutes

Serves 4

1 onion
1 clove garlic
250 g (8 oz) smoked ham
250 g (8 oz) open cup mushrooms
25 g (1 oz) butter
150 ml (5 fl oz) dry white wine
450 ml (15 fl oz) double cream
salt and freshly ground black pepper to taste
550 g (1 lb 2 oz) fresh spinach and ricotta tortellini
2 tablespoons freshly grated Parmesan cheese

My Brazilian friend Sandro is a lover of all things bad and when it comes to food, the richer and creamier the dish the better! His version of this dish combines spinach and ricotta tortellini with mushrooms, smoked ham, white wine, cream and Parmesan – it certainly lives up to his rich taste. The word *boscaiola* in an Italian dish indicates that it contains mushrooms in some form or other. Try this sauce with tagliatelle or fettucine if you prefer a lighter unfilled pasta.

1 Finely chop the onion and crush the garlic. Thinly slice the ham and mushrooms.
2 Melt the butter in a frying pan, add the onion and garlic and cook for 5 minutes, stirring occasionally, until the onion begins to soften. Add the ham and mushrooms and cook for 4 minutes, until the mushrooms are tender.
3 Stir in the wine and cream and season with plenty of ground black pepper. Bring to the boil, then lower the heat and simmer gently for 5 minutes until the sauce has reduced and begun to thicken.
4 Meanwhile bring a large saucepan of salted water to the boil, add the tortellini and cook according to packet instructions until tender, which should take about 5 minutes.
5 Drain the tortellini thoroughly and immediately return it to the pan. Add the sauce and Parmesan cheese and heat gently, tossing together until the tortellini is well coated. Transfer to warmed serving plates and serve at once.

SPAGHETTI ALLA PUTTANESCA

Time to make: 20 minutes
Time to cook: about 25 minutes

Serves 4

2 cloves garlic
1 small fresh red chilli
8 anchovy fillets
125 g (4 oz) pitted black olives
25 g (1 oz) butter
397 g (14 oz) can chopped tomatoes
salt and freshly ground black pepper to taste
400 g (14 oz) dried spaghetti
1 tablespoon capers
1 tablespooon chopped fresh parsley

*P*uttanesca literally translates as whore and this is the dish she would use to seduce her clients. While I can't promise guaranteed success as an aphrodisiac every time, I'm sure your partner will enjoy this rather piquant dish of spaghetti with tomatoes, capers, olives and anchovies.

1   Crush the garlic. Seed and chop the chilli very finely. Drain and finely chop the anchovy fillets and slice the olives.
2   Melt the butter in a frying pan, add the garlic, chilli and anchovies and cook for 1 minute, stirring. Add the tomatoes and a pinch of salt. Bring to the boil, then lower the heat and simmer gently uncovered for 10 minutes until the tomatoes have reduced and separated from the butter. Set aside.
3   Bring a large saucepan of salted water to the boil, add the spaghetti and cook according to packet instructions until tender, which should take about 15 minutes.
4   When the spaghetti is half cooked, return the sauce to the heat. Add the olives, capers and parsley and cook for 5 to 7 minutes, depending on your pasta.
5   Drain the spaghetti and immediately stir it into the sauce. Check seasoning and toss until the spaghetti is well coated with the sauce. Serve at once.

Cook's Tip
If you want to prepare this sauce in advance, follow steps 1 and 2 and leave to cool. Refrigerate until needed, then continue with steps 3, 4 and 5.

SPAGHETTI BOLOGNAISE

Time to make: 15 minutes
Time to cook: about 40 minutes

Serves 4

1 large onion

4 cloves garlic

2 tablespoons sunflower or olive oil

2 tablespoons dried mixed herbs

500 g (1 lb) minced beef

salt and freshly ground black pepper to taste

1 dessertspoon granulated sugar

4 tablespoons tomato ketchup

397 g (14 oz) can peeled plum tomatoes

350 g (12 oz) dried spaghetti

4 tablespoons grated Parmesan cheese to serve

This book would not be complete without my Mum's recipe for Spaghetti Bolognaise to which she subjected, or should I say treated, us every Wednesday as kids. It's similar to the classic Italian version in that the recipe is a simple meat sauce as opposed to some of the more modern recipes I have seen which include carrot, bacon, celery and mushrooms. My Mum swears by using tomato ketchup and says that the spoonful of sugar makes all the difference. I have to admit that even I haven't got bored with it yet! It keeps really well and tastes wonderful the day after it is made.

1 Roughly chop the onion and crush the garlic. Heat the oil in a large saucepan, add the onion, garlic and mixed herbs and cook for 5 minutes, stirring occasionally, until the onion begins to soften.
2 Add the minced beef, breaking it up with a wooden spoon, and a pinch of salt and cook, stirring occasionally, until browned.
3 Add the sugar, ketchup and tomatoes with their juice, breaking them up with a wooden spoon. Bring to the boil, stirring occasionally, then lower the heat, cover and simmer gently for 30 minutes. Check seasoning.
4 Meanwhile bring a large saucepan of salted water to the boil, add the spaghetti and cook according to packet instructions until tender, which should take about 15 minutes.
5 Drain the spaghetti and transfer to warmed serving plates. Spoon the meat sauce on top and sprinkle with the Parmesan cheese to serve.

Something special

I like nothing more than sitting around a table with family or friends eating, drinking and chatting, and I absolutely love cooking for people. These are my favourite dishes for entertaining. They are not difficult or expensive, just a bit different – it's amazing how much you can do with pasta.

PAPPARDELLE WITH SCALLOPS AND RED PEPPER SAUCE

Time to make: 20 minutes
Time to cook: about 20 minutes

Serves 4

2 red peppers

3 cloves garlic

40 g (1½ oz) fresh coriander

25 g (1 oz) pine kernels

25 g (1 oz) freshly grated Parmesan cheese

8 tablespoons extra-virgin olive oil

1 tablespoon balsamic vinegar

350 g (12 oz) dried pappardelle

500 g (1 lb) shelled scallops

1 teaspoon paprika

salt and freshly ground black pepper to taste

I went to the famous Seafood Restaurant in Padstow a couple of years ago and had a wonderful meal of fresh scallops with a red pepper sauce. It was so delicious that I decided to recreate the recipe as soon as I got home. I have since added a coriander pesto. Grilled pepper purée makes a superb pasta sauce – I have also served it with monkfish and mussels.

1 Preheat the grill to high. Halve, core and seed the peppers. Put the peppers and 2 unpeeled cloves garlic in the grill pan and grill for about 5 minutes, turning occasionally, until the skin is blackened and blistered. Remove from heat and put in a plastic bag for 2 minutes to loosen the skin. Leave grill on high.
2 Meanwhile set aside a few coriander leaves. Put the rest in a blender or food processor. Add the remaining garlic (peeled), pine kernels, Parmesan cheese and 5 tablespoons of the oil and process until smooth. Remove from the bowl and set aside. Wash the processor bowl and blade.
3 When cool enough to handle, peel the skin from the peppers and peel the grilled garlic. Put in the blender or food processor with the balsamic vinegar and 2 tablespoons of the oil and process until smooth. Transfer to a small saucepan and simmer gently, stirring occasionally.
4 Bring a large saucepan of salted water to the boil, add the pappardelle and cook according to packet instructions until tender, which should take 8 to 10 minutes.
5 Meanwhile line the grill pan with foil. Put the scallops in the pan and brush with the remaining oil. Sprinkle with the paprika and season with salt and ground black pepper. Grill for 4 to 5 minutes, turning once, until just firm. Slice each scallop in half or quarters, depending on their size, and add any juices from the pan to the pepper purée.
6 Drain the pappardelle thoroughly and immediately return it to the pan. Add the coriander pesto and toss together over low heat until the pappardelle is coated and the pesto has heated through. Add the scallops and toss gently to mix.
7 Transfer to warmed serving plates and pour over the warmed pepper sauce. Garnish with the reserved coriander leaves.

LINGUINI WITH CURRIED MUSSELS

Time to make: 30 minutes
Time to cook: about 30 minutes

Serves 4

1 kg (2 lb) mussels in shells
300 ml (10 fl oz) dry white wine
1 onion
25 g (1 oz) butter
1 teaspoon plain flour
1 teaspoon medium curry powder
400 g (14 oz) fresh linguini
142 ml (5 fl oz) carton double cream
salt and freshly ground black pepper to taste
finely snipped chives to garnish

This dish is really simple to make and always well received, providing of course your guests love mussels – although I have managed to convert a few food fusspots to their virtues via this dish. I think it's the lightly curried sauce that makes all the difference. If you can, buy Bouchot mussels as they contain no sand and need very little preparation .

1   Wash the mussels in several changes of cold water, scrub the shells and remove the beards. Discard any which do not close when firmly tapped.
2   Put the mussels in a large saucepan with the wine. Cover and cook over high heat for 5 minutes, shaking the pan occasionally, until the mussels have opened. Discard any that remain closed.
3   Meanwhile finely chop the onion. Bring a large saucepan of salted water to the boil and leave simmering.
4   Drain the mussels through a sieve and reserve the cooking liquid. Cut the mussels out of their shells and set aside.
5   Melt the butter in a large frying pan, add the onion and cook gently for 7 minutes, stirring occasionally, until softened. Stir in the flour and curry powder and cook for 3 minutes.
6   Carefully pour 450 ml (15 fl oz) of the reserved cooking liquid into the frying pan. Bring to the boil, stirring constantly until the sauce thickens slightly. Lower the heat and simmer for 10 minutes.
7   Add the linguini to the saucepan of boiling water and cook according to packet instructions until tender, which should take about 3 minutes.
8   Meanwhile return the mussels to the frying pan and add the cream. Season with salt and ground black pepper and simmer gently.
9   Drain the linguini and immediately return it to the pan. Add the mussels and sauce, tossing together until the linguini is well coated. Transfer to warmed serving plates and sprinkle with snipped chives to serve.

SPAGHETTI PESCATORE

Time to make: 15 minutes
Time to cook: about 15 minutes

Serves 4

500 g (1 lb) mussels in shells
12 large raw prawn tails
500 g (1 lb) squid
350 g (12 oz) monkfish tail, filleted
1 onion
2 cloves garlic
350 g (12 oz) dried spaghetti
50 g (2 oz) butter
150 ml (5 fl oz) dry white wine
3 tablespoons double cream
2 tablespoons chopped fresh parsley
salt and freshly ground black pepper to taste

Photographed on page 2

I lived on the coast in Devon until I was eighteen and was lucky enough to be brought up on fish fresh from the quay. For this dish I have used mussels, squid, prawns and monkfish. Ask your fishmonger to skin and fillet the monkfish tail for you as the skin is very tough and it isn't an easy job.

1   Wash the mussels in several changes of cold water. Scrub the shells and remove the beards. Discard any which do not close when firmly tapped. 'Butterfly' the prawns by cutting lengthways almost in half from the head end to tail, leaving the tail end intact. Set aside.
2   Wash the squid under running cold water and pull out the transparent quill. Slice into rings. Cut the monkfish into thin slices. Finely chop the onion and crush the garlic.
3   Bring a large saucepan of salted water to the boil, add the spaghetti and cook according to packet instructions until tender, which should take about 15 minutes.
4   Meanwhile melt 25 g (1 oz) of the butter in a large saucepan, add the onion and garlic and cook gently for 4 minutes until softened. Pour in the wine, increase the heat and bring to the boil.
5   Add the mussels and monkfish to the pan, cover and cook over high heat for 2 minutes. Add the prawns and squid and cook for a further 2 minutes until the mussels have opened. Remove the fish and shellfish with a slotted spoon, discarding any mussels that are still closed. Keep warm in a very low oven.
6   Bring the pan juices to the boil, then lower the heat and simmer until reduced by half. Add the cream, parsley and remaining butter. Season with ground black pepper and a little salt. Cook gently for 1 minute until the butter has melted.
7   Drain the spaghetti and immediately return it to the pan. Add the fish, shellfish and sauce and heat gently, tossing the mixture together. Serve at once.

TAGLIATELLE WITH SMOKED SALMON AND ASPARAGUS

Time to make: 15 minutes
Time to cook: 10 minutes

Serves 4

1 onion

175 g (6 oz) sliced smoked salmon

250 g (8 oz) asparagus tips

50 g (2 oz) butter

150 ml (5 fl oz) dry white wine

300 g (10 oz) dried paglia e fieno (green and yellow tagliatelle)

300 ml (10 fl oz) double cream

2 teaspoons creamed horseradish

2 tablespoons chopped fresh dill

salt and freshly ground black pepper to taste

dill fronds to garnish

Before my father retired, he was an antique dealer and did some rather extraordinary deals with his friends, including trading a watch in exchange for a side of smoked salmon. This, coupled with his love of asparagus, was how this recipe came about. Asparagus tips are available just about all year round now, but the short English season in May is when they're at their best.

1 Finely chop the onion. Cut the smoked salmon into 1 cm (½ in) strips.
2 Bring a large frying pan of salted water to the boil, add the asparagus tips and cook for 4 minutes until almost tender. Drain and cut into 5 cm (2 in) lengths. Set aside.
3 Melt the butter in the frying pan, add the onion and cook for 4 minutes over low heat, stirring occasionally, until golden. Stir in the wine, increase the heat and bring to the boil. Cook for 2 minutes until the wine has reduced by half.
4 Meanwhile bring a large saucepan of salted water to the boil, add the pasta and cook according to packet instructions until tender, which should take about 5 minutes.
5 Meanwhile stir the cream and horseradish into the wine and cook for 1 minute. Add the dill and season with salt and ground black pepper. One minute before the pasta is cooked, add the smoked salmon and asparagus to the wine sauce and simmer gently for 30 seconds. Remove from heat and set aside.
6 Drain the pasta thoroughly and add to the sauce, tossing gently to mix. Garnish with fronds of dill and serve at once.

Cook's Tip
Because of the slippery nature of smoked salmon, it is easier to cut into strips using scissors rather than a knife.

FRESH PASTA WITH SEAFOOD

Time to make: 5 minutes
Time to cook: about 5 minutes

Serves 4

250 g (8 oz) fresh cod or other white fish

4 fat cloves garlic

6 tablespoons extra-virgin olive oil

175 g (6 oz) small shelled scallops

175 g (6 oz) shelled mussels

175 g (6 oz) shelled prawns

4 tablespoons chopped fresh parsley

6 tablespoons lemon juice

salt and freshly ground black pepper to taste

400 g (14 oz) fresh trenette or linguini

This dish is the creation of Stephen Williams, chef at Piermasters restaurant in Plymouth where I worked for a year or so. Stephen has eaten many variations of this dish all over Italy, but the original for his version was made with mussels only, at a restaurant in Albissola Mare on the Savona Riviera. You can vary this dish with diced tomatoes and other herbs, especially basil, but whether it can be improved is another matter! Use thin noodles called trenette or fine spaghetti like linguini.

1 Cut the cod or other fish into 1 cm (½ in) pieces. Finely chop the garlic .
2 Bring a large saucepan of salted water to the boil and keep simmering.
3 Heat 3 tablespoons of the oil in a large frying pan. Add the cod, scallops, garlic, mussels and prawns and cook over high heat for 1 minute until the garlic is golden. Lower the heat.
4 Add the parsley, remaining oil and the lemon juice to the frying pan. Season with salt and ground black pepper and simmer gently for 30 seconds. Remove from heat and set aside.
5 Meanwhile add the trenette or linguini to the simmering water, bring to the boil and cook according to packet instructions until tender, which should take about 3 minutes.
6 Drain the pasta and immediately return it to the pan. Add the seafood and toss gently together until well mixed, taking care not to break up the fish. Check seasoning and serve at once with a crisp salad in a walnut oil dressing.

Cook's Tip
To chop garlic, crush the cloves under the blade of a knife. Pour over 1 teaspoon olive oil, sprinkle with a pinch of salt and chop finely. The oil will stop the garlic sticking to the knife

FARFALLE WITH GORGONZOLA

Time to make: 5 minutes
Time to cook: 10 to 15 minutes

Serves 4

500 g (1 lb) dried farfalle

125g (4 oz) gorgonzola

250 ml (8 fl oz) double cream

125 ml (4 fl oz) white wine

¼ teaspoon freshly grated nutmeg

salt and freshly ground black pepper to taste

snipped chives to garnish

Photographed on page 71

I lived in France for four months, working in an hotel, and on my weekly night off a crowd of us would religiously trundle through the snow to the one and only Italian restaurant in the resort, aptly named La Spaghetteria. It's from this restaurant that the recipe for Farfalle with Gorgonzola emerged. You could use any creamy blue cheese for this recipe but I like gorgonzola for its tangy taste and although it's not the cheapest of cheeses, a little goes a long way. The more cheese you add, the stronger the flavour.

1 Bring a large saucepan of salted water to the boil, add the farfalle and cook according to packet instructions until tender, which should take about 12 minutes.
2 Meanwhile crumble the gorgonzola. Five minutes before the farfalle is ready, pour the cream and wine into a separate saucepan. Add the gorgonzola and cook for 3 minutes, stirring constantly until the cheese has melted and the sauce is smooth.
3 Add the nutmeg and ground black pepper. Drain the farfalle and immediately return it to the pan. Add the sauce and toss until all the farfalle is well coated. Garnish with chives and serve at once.

Cook's Tip
Don't be tempted into cutting the rind off the gorgonzola – it melts perfectly into the sauce and adds to the flavour. For extra flavour, sprinkle with shredded basil and ground black pepper before serving.

LUMACONI CARBONARA WITH SMOKED HADDOCK AND PEAS

Time to make: 25 minutes
Time to cook: 10 to 15 minutes

Serves 4

---

500 g (1 lb) smoked haddock fillet, skinned

---

1 large onion

---

3 medium eggs, size 3

---

50 g (2 oz) freshly grated Parmesan cheese

---

2 tablespoons chopped fresh parsley

---

salt and freshly ground black pepper to taste

---

350 g (12 oz) dried lumaconi

---

40 g (1½ oz) butter

---

150 ml (5 fl oz) dry white wine

---

150 g (5 oz) frozen petit pois, thawed

---

flat-leaf parsley sprigs to garnish

Fish on Friday was a regular occurrence in the Watson household and my favourite was always smoked haddock with poached egg, peas and mashed potato. The combination of smoked haddock and peas was the inspiration for this recipe, together with an eggy carbonara sauce. I have used lumaconi pasta which are large snail shapes, but any large shell shaped pasta can be used.

1   Cut the haddock into 2.5 cm (1 in) cubes. Chop the onion.
2   Break the eggs into a mixing bowl large enough to hold the cooked pasta. Add the Parmesan cheese and parsley, reserving a little for garnish, and beat together. Season with salt and ground black pepper.
3   Bring a large saucepan of salted water to the boil, add the lumaconi and cook according to packet instructions until tender, which should take about 12 minutes.
4   Meanwhile melt the butter in a large frying pan, add the onion and cook for about 5 minutes until soft and golden. Stir in the wine and bring to the boil, then lower the heat and add the peas and haddock. Cover and cook for 2 to 3 minutes until the fish is firm. Season with salt and pepper, cover and remove from heat.
5   Drain the lumaconi thoroughly, then immediately add it to the egg mixture in the bowl. Toss well to cook the eggs until they are creamy. Add the haddock mixture and toss gently to mix. Sprinkle with the reserved parsley, garnish with parsley sprigs and serve at once.

Cook's Tip
Add the haddock mixture at the last minute and toss gently, taking care not to break up the fish. For a really creamy sauce, add 2 tablespoons cream to the egg mixture.

Top: Farfalle with Gorgonzola (see page 69)

Bottom: Lumaconi Carbonara with Smoked Haddock and Peas

TAGLIATELLE WITH CHICKEN LIVERS

Time to make: 20 minutes
Time to cook: 15 minutes

Serves 4

500 g (1 lb) chicken livers

1 small onion

1 clove garlic

1 thick slice pancetta (see Cook's Tip, page 57) or 3 slices unsmoked streaky bacon

25 g (1 oz) butter

3 tablespoons olive oil

4 tablespoons balsamic vinegar

salt and freshly ground black pepper to taste

2 tablespoons chopped fresh parsley

125 g (4 oz) frozen petit pois or peas, thawed

300 g (10 oz) dried tagliatelle

I am a huge fan of chicken livers. Their rich creamy flavour and the sweetness of peas marry perfectly with the simplicity of plain cooked pasta. Here they are tossed in a warm vinaigrette of olive oil and balsamic vinegar, which is wonderful mopped up with crusty granary bread.

1 Rinse and drain the chicken livers, then chop roughly, discarding any fibrous bit. Finely chop the onion and crush the garlic.
2 Remove the rind from the pancetta or bacon, then slice into small strips. Put in a frying pan and dry-fry for 4 minutes until lightly browned and just crisp. Remove from heat and set aside.
3 Melt the butter in a large pan, add the onion and garlic and cook for 5 minutes, stirring occasionally, until softened.
4 Meanwhile pour the oil and balsamic vinegar into a screw-top jar. Season well with salt and ground black pepper and shake well to mix. Set aside.
5 Increase the heat and add the chicken livers to the pan. Cook for 4 minutes until browned and sealed. Lower the heat and stir in the parsley, peas and half of the oil and vinegar mixture. Cook for 2 minutes, stirring occasionally.
6 Meanwhile bring a large saucepan of salted water to the boil, add the tagliatelle and cook according to packet instructions until tender, which should take about 5 minutes.
7 Drain the tagliatelle thoroughly and immediately return it to the pan. Add the chicken liver mixture, pancetta or bacon and remaining oil and vinegar mixture. Heat gently, tossing the mixture together until the tagliatelle is well coated. Check seasoning and transfer to warmed serving plates. Serve at once.

CAJUN CHICKEN RIGATONI WITH SALSA ROSSA

Time to make: 20 minutes
Time to cook: about 30 minutes

Serves 4

500 g (1 lb) skinned chicken breast fillets

3 cloves garlic

1 tablespoon paprika

½ teaspoon freshly ground black pepper

1 teaspoon ground cumin

1 teaspoon ground coriander

¼ teaspoon chilli powder

2 red peppers

1 fresh red chilli

2 onions

5 tablespoons olive oil

397 g (14 oz) can chopped tomatoes

½ teaspoon salt

350 g (12 oz) dried rigatoni

Ever since working in The Wilds restaurant in Fulham, where they served the most wonderful grilled chicken with salsa, I keep a jar of salsa in my fridge at all times. It keeps well and is great for an impromptu supper. Stored in a screw-top jar, it will keep for up to a month and makes a great accompaniment for grilled or cold meats. Here I have cooked it with spicy coated chicken tossed with rigatoni.

1 Cut the chicken into 1 cm (½ in) slices. Crush the garlic, putting 1 clove in a mixing bowl with the paprika, black pepper, cumin, coriander and chilli powder. Stir to mix, add the chicken and toss well to coat. Cover and set aside.
2 Preheat the grill to high. Put the red peppers in the grill pan and grill for 10 minutes, turning every 2 or 3 minutes, until the skin is blistered and blackened. Put in a plastic bag for 5 minutes to loosen the skin. Peel away the skin, halve, core and seed then roughly chop the flesh into 1 cm (½ in) pieces.
3 Meanwhile halve, seed and thinly slice the chilli, and finely chop the onions. Heat 4 tablespoons of the oil in a large frying pan, add the remaining garlic and the onion and cook gently for 6 minutes, stirring occasionally, until the onion has softened. Add the red peppers and chilli and cook gently for 10 minutes, stirring occasionally.
4 Add the tomatoes, bring to the boil, then lower the heat and simmer for 5 to 10 minutes, stirring occasionally, until the tomatoes have reduced by half. Spoon the mixture into a blender or food processor, add the salt and process until smooth. Set aside.
5 Meanwhile bring a large saucepan of salted water to the boil, add the rigatoni and cook according to packet instructions until tender, which should take about 13 minutes.
6 Meanwhile heat the remaining oil in a large pan, add the chicken and cook for 5 minutes, stirring occasionally, until tender.
7 Drain the rigatoni and immediately return it to the pan. Add the chicken and salsa and heat gently, tossing the mixture together until the rigatoni is well coated and the sauce has heated through. Serve at once.

Budget pasta

This chapter is a selection of cheap and cheerful recipes which don't skimp on flavour. In Italy pasta is a very inexpensive food, as they tend to serve a lot more pasta with a lot less sauce than we do. Most of the recipes are quick and easy, so they're ideal as home-from-work suppers. The Italian Meatballs and Bean Soup have become my staple diet at the end of each month, whilst waiting for pay day!

ITALIAN BEAN SOUP

Time to make: 20 minutes
Time to cook: 35 to 40 minutes

Serves 4

---

1 onion

2 carrots

2 cloves garlic

3 slices smoked streaky bacon

397 g (14 oz) can peeled plum tomatoes

2 beef stock cubes

1.4 litres (2½ pints) boiling water

397 g (14 oz) can borlotti beans

2 tablespoons oil

1 teaspoon dried thyme

¼ teaspoon salt

freshly ground black pepper to taste

125 g (4 oz) dried conchigliliette rigate or mini pasta shapes

4 tablespoons chopped fresh parsley

3 tablespoons freshly grated Parmesan cheese

In theory, the idea for this recipe comes from a traditional Italian peasant soup which uses dried beans, fresh beef stock, pancetta and fresh tomatoes. In practice, I have substituted canned beans for dried to save time, and used streaky bacon instead of pancetta and canned tomatoes instead of fresh to save money. You can use borlotti, kidney or white cannellini beans.

1 Roughly chop the onion and carrots and crush the garlic. Remove the rind from the bacon, then slice into thin strips. Put the canned tomatoes and their juice in a blender or food processor and process for 20 seconds until roughly chopped. Dissolve the stock cubes in the boiling water. Drain and rinse the beans.
2 Heat the oil in a large saucepan over low heat. Add the onion, carrot, garlic and bacon and cook for 10 to 15 minutes, stirring occasionally, until the vegetables have softened.
3 Add the thyme, salt and several grinds of black pepper. Stir in the stock, tomatoes and beans. Bring to the boil, then lower the heat and simmer uncovered for 15 minutes. Spoon half of the soup into the blender or food processor and process until smooth. Return to the pan with the pasta and 2 tablespoons of the parsley. Simmer uncovered for 10 minutes.
4 Check seasoning and stir in the remaining parsley. Transfer to warmed soup bowls and sprinkle with the Parmesan cheese to serve.

Sprinkling the soup with grated Parmesan cheese to serve

FUSILLI WITH BACON AND MUSHROOMS

Time to make: 10 minutes
Time to cook: 15 to 20 minutes

Serves 4

1 onion

1 clove garlic

125 g (4 oz) unsmoked streaky bacon

350 g (12 oz) button mushrooms

2 tablespoons sunflower oil

½ teaspoon ground nutmeg

1 tablespoon dried marjoram

salt and freshly ground black pepper to taste

350 g (12 oz) dried fusilli bucati corti

2 tablespoons freshly grated Parmesan cheese

When I was a student at Croydon college studying home economics, this pasta dish became my staple diet and I never got bored with it, although my landlady Eileen was fascinated by how unadventurous I was for someone supposedly studying food! Whenever possible I use fusilli bucati corti – the short springs that look like pieces of telephone cord – as they have a nice bite to them, but you could use fusilli, penne or rigatoni.

1   Finely chop the onion and crush the garlic. Remove the rind from the bacon, then chop into 2.5 cm (1 in) pieces. Slice the mushrooms.
2   Heat the oil in a frying pan, add the onion, garlic and bacon and cook for 5 minutes, stirring occasionally, until the onion begins to soften. Add the mushrooms, nutmeg and marjoram and season with salt and ground black pepper. Lower the heat, cover the pan with a tight-fitting lid and cook gently for a further 10 to 15 minutes.
3   Meanwhile bring a large saucepan of salted water to the boil, add the fusilli and cook according to packet instructions until tender, which should take about 12 minutes.
4   Drain the fusilli thoroughly and immediately return it to the pan. Add the mushroom mixture and Parmesan cheese and heat gently, tossing the mixture together until the pasta and sauce are well mixed. Serve at once.

Cook's Tip
Don't be fussy about following the recipe word for word – I have deviated from it many times. Use any type of mushroom you fancy, smoked bacon if you like and any herb. If you haven't got any nutmeg, use ground black pepper instead.

PENNE WITH TUNA AND PEAS

Time to make: 10 minutes
Time to cook: 15 to 20 minutes

Serves 4

350 g (12 oz) dried penne

175 g (6 oz) frozen petit pois

185 g (6½ oz) can tuna in brine

4 tablespoons mayonnaise

2 tablespoons lemon juice

1 tablespoon tomato ketchup

salt and freshly ground black pepper to taste

1 tablespoon chopped fresh parsley

You'll probably be surprised to find tomato ketchup and mayonnaise used as the basis for this dish, but I find they're the perfect storecupboard ingredients for a tuna sauce. This recipe belongs to Suzi, a friend with whom I've eaten this many times! I've used penne here but it works equally well with fusilli or rigatoni.

1   Bring a large saucepan of salted water to the boil, add the penne and cook according to packet instructions until tender, which should take about 12 minutes.
2   Meanwhile bring a separate saucepan of salted water to the boil. Add the peas, bring to the boil, then lower the heat and simmer for 2 minutes until tender. Drain and set aside.
3   Drain the tuna, spoon into a mixing bowl and mash with a fork. Add the mayonnaise, lemon juice and tomato ketchup and mix well to a creamy sauce. Season with plenty of ground black pepper.
4   Drain the penne and immediately return it to the pan. Add the tuna, peas and parsley and toss gently together until the penne is well coated with the sauce. Serve with a fresh spinach salad.

Cook's Tip
The heat from the cooked pasta and peas will heat the tuna sauce, so don't return it to the heat as it's likely to curdle.

VERMICELLI WITH BREADCRUMBS AND PARSLEY

Time to make: 5 minutes
Time to cook: about 10 minutes

Serves 4

1 large onion

2 cloves garlic

8 tablespoons olive oil

250 g (8 oz) dried vermicelli

50 g (2 oz) fresh white breadcrumbs

6 tablespoons chopped fresh parsley

salt and freshly ground black pepper to taste

8 tablespoons freshly grated Parmesan cheese

It's great working in the cookery department of magazines as there are always recipes being tested which need to be tasted. Coralie Dorman, cookery editor of Me magazine, developed this recipe for a pasta feature. The secret of its success lies in its simplicity.

1   Finely chop the onion and crush the garlic.
2   Heat the oil in a large frying pan, add the onion and garlic and cook for 5 minutes, stirring occasionally, until the onion has softened.
3   Bring a large saucepan of salted water to the boil, add the vermicelli and cook according to packet instructions until tender, which should take 2 to 3 minutes.
4   Meanwhile add the breadcrumbs and parsley to the onions and fry for 3 minutes until golden. Season with salt and ground black pepper.
5   Drain the vermicelli and immediately return it to the pan. Add the breadcrumb mixture and Parmesan cheese and heat gently, tossing together until well mixed. Serve with a fresh spinach salad and crusty bread.

Cook's Tips
Adjust the amount of vermicelli according to appetite. As it is so fine, a small quantity in weight cooks to a huge amount. Wholemeal breadcrumbs work equally well and look more attractive.

Top: Spaghetti with Fresh Tomato Sauce (see page 80)

Bottom: Vermicelli with Breadcrumbs and Parsley

SPAGHETTI WITH FRESH TOMATO SAUCE

Time to make: 15 minutes
Time to cook: 30 minutes

Serves 4

500 g (1 lb) ripe tomatoes

1 onion

1 large carrot

1 stick celery

2 cloves garlic

3 tablespoons sunflower or olive oil

1 tablespoon tomato purée

2 bay leaves

1 teaspoon sugar

1 teaspoon dried oregano

1 teaspoon dried basil

salt and freshly ground black pepper to taste

300 g (10 oz) dried spaghetti

Photographed on page 79

Ripe English tomatoes really bring home the pleasure of eating within the seasons. As far as I'm concerned they're only worth eating during the summer when they're ripe and full of flavour and also at their cheapest. This tomato sauce is one of my favourite standbys. It's delicious in its own right but can also be used as the base for other sauces or as a pizza topping. Make it in large quantities and freeze in batches.

1   Cut a cross in the top of each tomato and put in a large mixing bowl. Cover with boiling water and leave for 30 seconds until the skins begin to split, then remove with a slotted spoon. Carefully peel away the skin, halve, seed and roughly chop the flesh.
2   Finely chop the onion, carrot and celery and crush the garlic. Heat the oil in a saucepan, add the onion, carrot, celery and garlic and cook over low heat for 5 minutes, stirring occasionally, until the vegetables have softened
3   Stir in the tomatoes, tomato purée, bay leaves, sugar, oregano and basil and season with salt and ground black pepper. Cover and simmer gently for 15 minutes, stirring occasionally.
4   Remove the lid from the pan and simmer uncovered for a further 10 minutes until the vegetables are tender. Discard the bay leaves.
5   Meanwhile bring a large saucepan of salted water to the boil, add the spaghetti and cook according to packet instructions until tender, which should take about 15 minutes.
6   Drain the spaghetti and immediately return it to the pan. Add the tomato sauce and heat gently, tossing the mixture together until the spaghetti is well coated. Check seasoning and serve at once.

Cook's Tip
To freeze the sauce, leave to cool completely then transfer to a rigid container, cover and freeze for up to one month. To use, reheat slowly from frozen.

PENNE WITH RED PESTO AND SOURED CREAM

Time to make: 5 minutes
Time to cook: 10 to 15 minutes

Serves 2

175 g (6 oz) dried penne

142 ml (5 fl oz) carton fresh soured cream

3 tablespoons red pesto sauce

salt and freshly ground black pepper to taste

snipped chives to garnish

Before I bought my own flat last year I shared with a friend called Chloe, who has a very concise library of recipes – two to be precise! Roasted pepper soup is the first and the second is this simple pasta dish which we have eaten many a time, accompanied by a bottle of wine.

1 Bring a large saucepan of salted water to the boil, add the penne and cook according to packet instructions until tender but not quite cooked, which should take about 10 minutes. (The pasta will finish cooking in the sauce.)
2 Meanwhile pour the soured cream into a small mixing bowl, add the red pesto sauce and mix well. Season with a generous amount of ground black pepper.
3 Drain the penne and immediately return it to the pan. Add the pesto sauce and heat gently for 2 minutes, tossing the mixture together, until the sauce has heated through.
4 Transfer to warmed serving plates and sprinkle with snipped chives. Serve with a crisp green, or avocado and tomato, salad.

PIPE RIGATE WITH RATATOUILLE

Time to make: 15 minutes
Time to cook: 40 minutes

Serves 4

1 large onion

2 cloves garlic

350 g (12 oz) fresh tomatoes or 397 g (14 oz) can chopped tomatoes

1 red pepper

1 yellow pepper

250 g (8 oz) aubergines

250 g (8 oz) courgettes

3 tablespoons olive oil

1 tablespoon tomato purée

1 bouquet garni

salt and freshly ground black pepper to taste

2 tablespoons chopped fresh oregano or 2 teaspoons dried

350 g (12 oz) dried pipe rigate

oregano sprigs to garnish

Parmesan cheese shavings to serve (see page 28)

Pipe are large elbow-shaped pasta tubes, available plain or with a ribbed 'rigate' surface. Their design enables them to take up large quantities of sauce and they work particularly well with chunks of chicken, meat or vegetables. This chunky ratatouille is one of the most versatile dishes ever. It makes a great starter, hot or cold, can be served as an accompaniment to meat or fish and is wonderful stirred through pasta. Although the vegetables used in ratatouille are now available all year round, I prefer to eat them in their summer season when they are at their cheapest and best.

1   Slice the onion and crush the garlic. Roughly chop the tomatoes if using fresh. Halve, core and seed the red and yellow peppers, then cut into 2.5 cm (1 in) squares. Trim and roughly chop the aubergines into 1 cm (½ in) chunks. Cut the courgettes into 1 cm (½ in) slices, then cut the slices in half.
2   Heat the oil in a large frying pan, add the onion and garlic and cook gently for 5 minutes until soft and golden. Add the peppers aubergines and courgettes and cook gently, stirring occasionally, for a further 10 minutes. Add the fresh or canned tomatoes, tomato purée and bouquet garni and season with salt and ground black pepper. Cover and simmer for 15 minutes.
3   Add the oregano and cook uncovered for a further 10 minutes until the liquid has reduced and the vegetables are soft. Remove the bouquet garni.
4   Meanwhile bring a large saucepan of salted water to the boil, add the pipe rigate and cook according to packet instructions until tender, which should take 10 to 12 minutes. Drain the pasta and immediately return it to the pan. Add the ratatouille and toss together over low heat until the pasta is well coated with the sauce. Garnish with oregano and serve with Parmesan cheese shavings.

GHAẞINA

Time to make: 5 minutes
Time to cook: about 15 minutes

Serves 2

175 g (6 oz) dried spaghetti

15 g (½ oz) butter

**2 teaspoons Bovril® or
Marmite®**

Ghaẞina, literally meaning pasta, is a traditional Maltese peasant dish made simply of pasta, butter and Bovril®. I first tasted it when I was sharing a flat in Plymouth with a friend called Vanessa, whose mother is Maltese. It went on to become a staple hangover cure, as I found that if you eat it late at night you don't suffer a hangover in the morning. Another great thing about it is that the recipe has only three ingredients – which you might well have in your kitchen – and it's not too taxing to make, which is important in the early hours of the morning! It's also better for you than a kebab on the way home!

1 Break the spaghetti into roughly 2.5 cm (1 in) lengths. Bring a large saucepan of water to the boil, add the spaghetti and cook according to packet instructions until tender, which should take about 15 minutes.
2 Drain the spaghetti in a sieve, not a colander as it might fall through the holes, and return it to the pan. Add the butter and Bovril® or Marmite® and toss together well until the butter has melted and the spaghetti is well coated. Enjoy!

Cook's Tips
Don't salt the water for the pasta, as Marmite® and Bovril® are salty enough.
If you are lucky you can buy quick-cook spaghetti which takes only 5 minutes to cook – it's completely changed my life !

SPAGHETTI WITH ITALIAN MEATBALLS

Time to make: 30 minutes
Time to cook: 1 hour 10 minutes

Serves 6

2 slices of white bread

5 tablespoons milk

1 onion

1 carrot

2 cloves garlic

500 g (1 lb) lean minced beef

1 egg

2 tablespoons freshly grated Parmesan cheese

2 tablespoons chopped fresh parsley

salt and freshly ground black pepper to taste

2 tablespoons olive oil

¼ teaspoon crushed chillies

1 tablespoon dried mixed herbs

1 tablespoon tomato purée

2 x 397 g (14 oz) cans peeled plum tomatoes

500 g (1 lb) dried spaghetti

freshly grated Parmesan cheese to serve

This was one of the first recipes I ever cooked in domestic science at school. I went on to have the more authentic version in St Marks Square in Venice. The mistake that is often made with this recipe is making the meatballs too large, which results in them being tough and chewy. They should be no bigger than the average conker and should be left cooking in the zesty tomato sauce for about an hour so that they are moist and tender.

1   Put the bread in a large bowl, add the milk and leave to soak for 10 minutes. Meanwhile finely chop the onion and carrot and crush the garlic.
2   When the bread has soaked up all the milk, add the minced beef, egg, Parmesan cheese and parsley. Season with a generous amount of salt and ground black pepper. Knead well to combine.
3   Divide the mixture into 32 pieces and shape into 2.5 cm (1 in) balls. Heat the oil in a large frying pan, add the meatballs and cook over high heat for 4 minutes, turning occasionally, until browned. Remove from the pan with a slotted spoon and set aside.
4   Add the onion, carrot and garlic to the pan and cook for 4 minutes, stirring occasionally, until the vegetables begin to soften. Stir in the crushed chillies and mixed herbs and cook for 30 seconds. Transfer the mixture to a large saucepan. Add the tomato purée and canned tomatoes with their juice, stirring to break up the tomatoes. Add the meat balls and bring to the boil, then lower the heat, cover and simmer for 1 hour. Season with salt and ground black pepper.
5   After 45 minutes, bring a large saucepan of salted water to the boil, add the spaghetti and cook according to packet instructions until tender, which should take about 15 minutes.
6   Drain the spaghetti and immediately return it to the pan. Add the sauce and toss well to mix. Transfer to warmed serving plates and serve with grated Parmesan cheese.

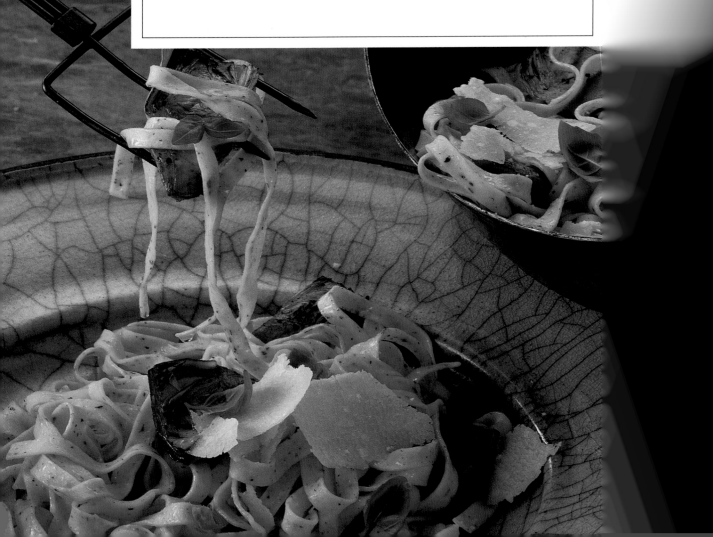

Party pasta

Like a good casserole, a baked pasta dish is an ideal choice when catering for large numbers, as more often than not it can be made in advance, leaving you more time to enjoy the party and less time in the kitchen. All the recipes in this chapter serve 8 and can be doubled or trebled as required. Those that can't be made in advance require a minimal amount of last-minute preparation and cooking.

GARLIC AND HERB TAGLIATELLE WITH ANTIPASTO

Time to make: 5 minutes
Time to cook: 5 to 10 minutes

Serves 8

800 g (1 lb 10 oz) fresh tagliatelle with garlic and herbs

75 g (3 oz) Parmesan cheese

4 tablespoons basil leaves

4 tablespoons olive oil

2 x 290 g (10 oz) jars antipasto artichokes

salt and freshly ground black pepper to taste

This recipe is a bit of a cheat really, but has saved me on many occasions. I remember being held up at a food photography session where I had been cooking all day. I was expecting a crowd round for supper and had about an hour in which to get home and prepare some food. I'd had just about enough of cooking that day, so ran into a supermarket and looked for the easiest thing to prepare – this was the result. Fresh pasta tossed with a jar of antipasto and Parmesan cheese. No one knew that I hadn't been slaving away all evening – I can highly recommend it!

1 Bring one large saucepan or two smaller saucepans of salted water to the boil, add the tagliatelle and cook according to packet instructions until tender, which should take about 4 minutes.
2 Meanwhile, using a potato peeler pare the Parmesan cheese into shavings and set aside. Shred most of the basil, reserving a few leaves for garnish.
3 Drain the tagliatelle and immediately return it to the pan. Add the oil, artichokes and shredded basil. Season with salt and ground black pepper and toss together over low heat for 3 minutes until the artichokes are heated through.
4 Transfer to warmed serving plates and top with the Parmesan cheese shavings and remaining basil leaves. Serve at once.

Cook's Tip
Antipasto is traditionally served as a starter in Italy, but it works really well as a pasta sauce. I have used artichokes in this recipe but I have also made this dish with other varieties of antipasto, including antipasto with mushrooms and antipasto pepperoni condiverdi – mixed peppers – which are also ideal.

CHICKEN AND SPINACH LASAGNE

Time to make: 1 hour
Time to cook: 2¼ to 2½ hours

Serves 8 to 10

1 carrot

1 onion

2 kg (4 lb) oven-ready chicken

3 bay leaves

salt and freshly ground black pepper to taste

250 g (8 oz) frozen chopped spinach, thawed

500 g (1 lb) chestnut mushrooms

2 fat cloves garlic

175 g (6 oz) gruyère cheese

50 g (2 oz) fresh white breadcrumbs

175 g (6 oz) butter

2 tablespoons lemon juice

125 g (4 oz) plain flour

1 litre (35 fl oz) milk

150 g (5 oz) cream cheese with garlic and herbs

3 tablespoons chopped fresh tarragon

300 g (10 oz) quick-cook lasagne

Don't be put off by the length of this recipe – the time and effort it takes are worth the compliments which follow.

1   Roughly chop the carrot and quarter the onion. Put the chicken in a large saucepan, cover with cold water and add the carrot, onion and bay leaves. Season with salt and ground black pepper. Bring to the boil, then lower the heat, cover and simmer for 1 hour until the chicken is cooked. Transfer the chicken to a plate and leave to cool. Reserve the cooking liquid and vegetables.
2   Meanwhile put the spinach in a metal sieve and drain well. Transfer to a bowl. Quarter the mushrooms and crush the garlic. Grate the gruyère cheese into a mixing bowl and stir in the breadcrumbs. Butter a 36 x 25 cm (14 x 10 in) ovenproof dish.
3   Remove the flesh from the chicken and cut into bite-size pieces. Return the skin and bones to the reserved cooking liquid. Bring to the boil and reduce by half until you are left with about 1 litre (35 fl oz) stock. Skim off the fat, strain and reserve the stock.
4   Melt 50 g (2 oz) of the butter in a large saucepan, add the mushrooms, lemon juice and seasoning. Cover and cook for 4 minutes, stirring occasionally, until the mushrooms are tender. Remove with a slotted spoon and set aside. Increase the heat to evaporate any water so that there is only butter left in the pan.
5   Melt the remaining butter in the same pan. Carefully stir in the flour and cook for 1 minute, then slowly blend in the reserved stock and the milk. Bring to the boil, stirring constantly, then lower the heat and simmer for 2 minutes, stirring occasionally. Remove from heat and stir in the cream cheese, garlic, tarragon and spinach. Season with salt and ground black pepper.
6   Set the oven to 200C, 400F, Gas 6. Spoon enough of the sauce into the prepared dish to cover the base. Top with a layer of lasagne. Sprinkle with 1 teaspoon water and cover with a layer of chicken and mushrooms. Repeat the layers, finishing with sauce and making sure it completely covers the ingredients underneath.
7   Sprinkle with the cheese and breadcrumb mixture. Put the dish on a baking sheet and cook on the centre shelf of the oven for 1 to 1¼ hours, until well browned. Cover with foil halfway through cooking if the topping begins to burn.

ORECCHIETTE WITH SPINACH AND HAZELNUTS

Time to make: 10 minutes
Time to cook: about 15 minutes

Serves 8 as a starter

1 clove garlic

125 g (4 oz) button mushrooms

50 g (2 oz) Parmesan cheese

125 g (4 oz) frozen chopped spinach, thawed

350 g (12 oz) dried orecchiette

1 tablespoon olive oil

salt and freshly ground black pepper to taste

142 ml (5 fl oz) carton double cream

1 tablespoon lemon juice

½ teaspoon freshly grated nutmeg

25 g (1 oz) roasted chopped hazelnuts

This dish is the creation my friend Penny, who is a very good cook and the perfect hostess. She has the enviable ability to make something from nothing and it always tastes excellent. The wonderful contrast in colour between the spinach and pasta together with the flavour of roasted hazelnuts and nutmeg make this dish a real dinner-party success. I prefer to serve it as a starter as it's quite rich and could be too much as a main course.

1   Crush the garlic and slice the mushrooms. Using a potato peeler, pare the Parmesan cheese into shavings. Drain the spinach in a sieve, pressing with the back of a wooden spoon to extract all the liquid.

2   Bring a large saucepan of salted water to the boil, add the orecchiette and cook according to packet instructions until tender, which should take about 14 minutes.

3   Meanwhile heat the oil in a large frying pan, add the garlic and a pinch of salt and cook for 3 minutes until golden.

4   Add the mushrooms and cook for 4 minutes, stirring occasionally. Stir in the spinach, cream, lemon juice and nutmeg. Bring to the boil, then lower the heat and simmer gently for 2 minutes. Season with salt and ground black pepper.

5   Drain the orecchiette and immediately return it to the pan. Add the spinach mixture and hazelnuts and toss together until the orecchiette is well coated. Transfer to warmed serving plates and top with the Parmesan cheese shavings.

Cook's Tip
To clean mushrooms, wipe them with a damp piece of absorbent kitchen paper.

CAMPANELLE WITH CHICK PEAS

Time to make: 15 minutes
Time to cook: 25 minutes

Serves 8 as a starter

2 onions

2 carrots

4 cloves garlic

2 sticks celery

3 tablespoons olive oil

1 teaspoon crushed chillies

397 g (14 oz) can chick peas

397 g (14 oz) can chopped tomatoes

2 tablespoons tomato purée

salt and freshly ground black pepper to taste

350 g (12 oz) dried campanelle

75 g (3 oz) freshly grated Parmesan cheese

Garnish

rosemary sprigs

extra freshly grated Parmesan cheese

This spicy tomato sauce with chick peas and Parmesan is one of those starters that you can depend on time and time again and never get bored with. It actually tastes better the day after it is made so I tend to make it the night before I serve it. The first time I made it, I used ditali – small macaroni-shape pasta – but I have never been able to get it since. I now use egg campanelle, which are small fluted dried pasta shapes. Ordinary macaroni works equally well too.

1 Finely chop the onions, carrots, garlic and celery.
2 Heat the oil in a large flameproof casserole, add the onion, carrot, garlic, celery and crushed chillies and cook over low heat for 10 minutes, stirring occasionally, until the vegetables have softened. Meanwhile drain the chick peas.
3 Add the chick peas, tomatoes and tomato purée to the pan, bring to the boil, then lower the heat and simmer uncovered for 5 minutes until the sauce has reduced and thickened. Cover and simmer for a further 10 minutes. Season with ground black pepper.
4 Meanwhile bring a large saucepan of salted water to the boil, add the campanelle and cook according to packet instructions until tender, which should take about 12 minutes.
5 Drain the campanelle and stir it into the sauce with the Parmesan cheese. Check seasoning and stir gently together until well mixed. Garnish with rosemary and extra Parmesan cheese and serve at once.

Cook's Tip
Do not add salt until right at the end as Parmesan cheese is salty. If you want to make this sauce in advance, follow steps 1 to 3, leave the sauce to cool, then cover and store in the fridge. Reheat the sauce over low heat 20 minutes before you want to serve and continue with steps 4 and 5.

TUNA PASTA BAKE

Time to make: 35 minutes
Time to cook: about 25 minutes

Serves 8

2 onions

2 cloves garlic

5 cm (2 in) piece fresh root ginger

2 tablespoons chilli oil

550 g (1 lb 2 oz) dried wholewheat riccioli (twists)

150 ml (5 fl oz) dry white wine or cider

2 teaspoons cornflour

2 x 397 g (14 oz) cans chopped tomatoes

2 tablespoons tomato purée

1 tablespoon lemon juice

2 tablespoons Worcestershire sauce

2 tablespoons brown fruity sauce

salt and freshly ground black pepper to taste

2 x 185 g (6½ oz) cans tuna in brine

325 g (11½ oz) can sweetcorn

2 x 227 g (8 oz) cans water chestnuts

4 tomatoes

350 g (12 oz) Cheddar cheese

This dish is great – it's quick and easy to make, filling and doesn't cost the earth. The root ginger and water chestnuts add a slightly oriental flavour to what would otherwise be a standard tuna and tomato concoction.

1   Chop the onions, crush the garlic and peel and finely chop the ginger. Heat the oil in a large saucepan, add the onion, garlic and ginger and fry for about 5 minutes, stirring occasionally, until they begin to soften.
2   Meanwhile bring a large saucepan of salted water to the boil, add the riccioli and cook according to packet instructions until tender, which should take 10 to 12 minutes.
3   Measure the wine or cider into a jug, add the cornflour and blend until smooth. Add to the onion mixture with the canned tomatoes, tomato purée, lemon juice, Worcestershire sauce, brown fruity sauce and salt and ground black pepper. Bring to the boil, then lower the heat and simmer uncovered for 2 minutes.
4   Drain the tuna, sweetcorn and water chestnuts. Cut the water chestnuts into quarters. Add the tuna, sweetcorn and water chestnuts to the tomato mixture and stir until well mixed.
5   Drain the riccioli and immediately stir it into the tomato sauce. Check seasoning.
6   Set the oven to 200C, 400F, Gas 6. Thinly slice the tomatoes and grate the Cheddar cheese. Stir 75 g (3 oz) of the cheese into the riccioli mixture. Spoon into a shallow 25 x 36 cm (10 x 14 in) ovenproof dish or two smaller dishes. Arrange the sliced tomatoes on top and sprinkle with the remaining cheese.
7   Put the dish on a baking sheet and cook on the top shelf of the oven for 10 to 15 minutes until the cheese is bubbling and golden. Serve with a crisp green salad and garlic bread if your guests are really hungry.

Cook's Tip
Instead of bringing a saucepan of water to the boil, you can boil the water in a kettle for cooking the pasta.

SPAGHETTINI WITH GREEN CURRY

Time to make: 30 minutes
Time to cook: 1 hour 10 minutes

Serves 8

900 g (2 lb) skinned chicken breast fillets

2 teaspoons salt

2 large onions

2 cloves garlic

5 cm (2 in) piece fresh root ginger

1 large green pepper

1 large yellow pepper

4 tablespoons oil

2 tablespoons Thai green curry paste

900 ml (30 fl oz) unsweetened coconut milk

625 g (1 lb 4 oz) dried spaghettini

I spent a month travelling through Thailand with a friend called Bridget and had one of the best green curries I've ever tasted, cooked by the locals, in a wooden hut high up in the hills of Chiang Mai. I've borrowed the idea for this pasta dish from the green curry recipe that Bridget has since created, although I have to admit to using green curry paste instead of starting from scratch with fresh lemon grass and chilli. We had it served with padthai (fried noodles) but it's equally good tossed with spaghettini (very fine spaghetti) or trenette (fine noodles).

1 Cut the chicken into 1 cm (½ in) pieces. Sprinkle with the salt and set aside. Finely chop the onions, garlic and ginger. Cut the peppers into quarters, remove the core and seeds, then cut into 1 cm (½ in) strips widthways .
2 Heat the oil in a large flameproof casserole, add the onion, garlic, ginger and peppers and stir-fry for 3 minutes until just beginning to brown .
3 Stir in the curry paste and cook for 2 minutes, stirring occasionally. Add the chicken and cook for 4 minutes until white.
4 Stir in the coconut milk, bring to the boil, then lower the heat, cover and simmer for 1 hour.
5 After 45 minutes, bring one very large saucepan or two smaller saucepans of salted water to the boil. Add the spaghettini and cook according to packet instructions until tender, which should take 10 to 12 minutes.
6 Drain the spaghettini and return it to the pan. Add the chicken and sauce and toss together gently until the spaghettini is well coated. Serve at once.

Cook's Tips
This sauce reheats well. If you want to make it in advance, follow steps 1 to 4 but simmer for only 45 minutes. Leave to cool, then chill until required. Bring back to the boil, then lower the heat, cover and simmer for 15 minutes while continuing with steps 5 and 6.
Thai green curry paste is available from delicatessens and oriental stores, and some leading supermarkets.

SPICY LAMB BAKE

Time to make: 25 minutes
Time to cook: 40 to 45 minutes

Serves 8

2 large onions

4 tablespoons olive oil

625 g (1 lb 4 oz) minced lamb

2 x 397 g (14 oz) cans chopped tomatoes

½ teaspoon ground cinnamon

3 tablespoons chopped fresh oregano

salt and freshly ground black pepper to taste

625 g (1 lb 4 oz) dried macaroni

175 g (6 oz) Emmental cheese

175 g (6 oz) wholemeal breadcrumbs

flat-leaf parsley and oregano sprigs to garnish

I always imagine serving this in a big rustic earthenware pot outdoors on a scrubbed wooden table with lots of crusty bread and a simple salad. In reality the weather has never been up to much when I've decided to cook it! That aside, it is a peasant-type dish that always goes down well with friends even though it's not particularly smart.

1 Roughly chop the onions. Heat the oil in a large frying pan, add the onion and cook for 4 minutes, stirring occasionally, until beginning to soften.
2 Add the lamb and cook over high heat for 3 minutes until sealed and browned. Add the tomatoes, cinnamon and chopped oregano and season with salt and ground black pepper. Bring to the boil, then lower the heat and simmer uncovered for 10 minutes. Cover and simmer for a further 5 minutes. Remove from heat and set aside.
3 Meanwhile bring a large saucepan of salted water to the boil, add the macaroni and cook according to packet instructions until tender, which should take 10 to 12 minutes. Drain thoroughly and stir into the meat sauce.
4 While the macaroni and lamb are cooking, grate the Emmental cheese into a mixing bowl. Stir in the breadcrumbs. Grease the base and sides of a 3.5 litre (6 pint) ovenproof dish.
5 Set the oven to 200C, 400F, Gas 6. Spoon the lamb and macaroni mixture into the prepared dish and sprinkle with the cheese and breadcrumb mixture. Bake on the centre shelf of the oven for 20 minutes until golden brown and bubbling. Cover with foil if the top begins to burn. Garnish with parsley and oregano and serve with crusty bread and a mixed leaf salad. Olives make a good accompaniment too – if you like them!

INDEX